Talk French

Isabelle Fournier

Series editor
Alwena Lamping

Published by BBC Worldwide Ltd
Woodlands, 80 Wood Lane, London W12 0TT
Revised and updated 2002
Reprinted 2003 (3 times), 2004, 2005

© BBC Worldwide Ltd 1998
ISBN 0 563 400684

Developed by BBC Languages
Edited by Geraldine Sweeney
Additional editing by Jenny Gwynne; Tara Dempsey
Design management by Book Creation Services
Design by Avril Broadley for BCS
Illustrations by Avril Broadley, Sylvie Rabbe for BCS
Typeset by Gene Ferber for BCS
Production controller Christopher Tinker
Cover design by Carroll Associates
Cover photographs The Stock Market (tr); David Noble (tl);
    Getty Images (b, back)
Audio producer John Green, TEFL tapes
Presenters Marianne Borgo; Stephane Cornicard; Philippe Monnet;
    Vanessa Seydoux
Sound engineer Tim Woolf
Studio Robert Nichols Audio Productions
Music by Peter Hutchings

Printed and bound in Great Britain by Martins the Printers Ltd,
    Berwick-upon-Tweed

Contents

Introduction

Welcome to **Talk French**, the BBC's new French course for absolute beginners. Designed for adults, learning at home or in a class, it provides the ideal introduction to French, covering the basic language needed in everyday situations on a visit to France. It is suitable if you want to learn for work, for fun or in order to prepare for a first level qualification.

Talk French is an interactive course consisting of a book and two 60-minute audio cassettes or CDs made by native French speakers. Although designed to be used with the audio, the book could be used separately, as audio scripts are included in the reference section. Free tutors support and activities are available online at http://www.bbcworldwide.com/talk.

Talk French encourages you to make genuine progress and promotes a real sense of achievement. The key to its effectiveness lies in its structure and its systematic approach. Key features include:

- simple step-by-step presentation of new language
- involvement and interaction at every stage of the learning process
- regular progress checks
- useful hints on study skills and language learning strategies

How to use Talk French

Each of the ten units is completed in ten easy-to-follow steps.

1   Read the first page of the unit to focus on what you are aiming to learn and to note any key vocabulary in the *En France* section. This provides useful and relevant information on France and sets your learning in context.

2   Listen to the key phrases on the audio – don't be tempted to read them first. Then listen to them again, this time reading them in your book too. Finally, try reading them out loud before listening one more time.

3   Work your way, step by step, through the activities which follow the key phrases. These highlight key language elements and are carefully designed to develop

your listening skills and your understanding of French. When you hear the activity number, pause the audio and read the instructions before you listen. To check your answers, refer to the *Audio scripts and answers* starting on page 99.

4   Read the *En français* explanations of how the language works as you come to them – they are placed just where you need that information.

5   When you have completed the activities, and before you try the *Put it all together* section, close your book and listen to the French conversations straight through. The more times you listen, the more familiar the language will become and the more comfortable you will become with it. You might also like to read the dialogues at this stage.

6   Complete the consolidation activities on the *Put it all together* page and check your answers with the *Audio scripts and answers*.

7   Use the language you've learnt – the presenters on the audio will prompt you and guide you through the *Now you're talking!* page as you practise speaking French.

8   Check your progress. First, test your knowledge with the quiz. Then check whether you can do everything on the checklist – if in doubt, go back and spend some more time on the relevant section. You'll have further opportunities to test your knowledge in each *Contrôle* after units 4, 7 and 10.

9   Read the learning hint at the end of the unit, which provides ideas and suggestions on how to use your study time effectively or how to extend your knowledge.

10 Finally, relax and listen to the whole unit, understanding what the people are saying in French and taking part in the conversations. This time you may not need the book, so you can listen to the audio on its own.

Bonne chance! Good luck!

Pronunciation guide

The best way to acquire a good French accent is to listen as often as you can to the speakers on the audio and imitate them closely. You will notice that French contains several nasal sounds not used in English, which can only be learnt by listening and imitating.

1 Vowels

French vowels sound approximately like the sounds in these English words:

a	e/eu	é	è/ê	ai
hat	fur	café	air	met
i/y	**o/au/eau**	**oi**	**u**	**ou**
pit	paw, gâteau	swan	tutu	fool

2 Consonants

as in . . .

c	+ e or i, and ç	centre, ici, ça va?	Celia
	+ other letters	Canada, combien	kilo
ch		chambre, marché	sugar
g	+ e or i	étage, gîte	leisure
	+ other letters	garage, gramme	get
gn		campagne	onion
h		j'habite, hôtel	(silent)
qu	(like k)	que, quiche	kilo
ll	(usually)	elle, ville	until
	(sometimes)	fille, je travaille	yacht

In French, you pronounce **j**, **b**, **d**, **p**, **t** more softly than in English while **r** is rolled more, like a Scottish **r**.

3

Usually in French, the final consonant of a word is not sounded:

chat is pronounced **cha.**
chaud is pronounced **chau.**

. . . unless the following word starts with a vowel or silent h:

Vous habitez en France? (Pronounced Vou**z**abitez en France?)
Il est anglais. (Pronounced Il es**t**anglais.)

Bonjour! Ça va?

- **saying hello and goodbye**
- **asking someone's name**
- **introducing yourself**
- **using the numbers 0 to 10**

En France . . . (In France . . .)

greeting people and saying goodbye are often accompanied by a handshake. Close friends and relatives kiss each other on both cheeks – two, three or four times depending on local custom. When greeting someone it is usual to add their name.

When talking to someone you don't know, you address a man as **monsieur** and a woman as **madame**, or **mademoiselle** if she is very young. Followed by a surname, these words are the equivalent of Mr, Mrs and Miss and, in writing, they are usually abbreviated to **M.**, **Mme** and **Mlle**.

Saying hello . . .

1 Listen to these key phrases.

Bonjour	Hello/Good morning/ Good afternoon
Bonsoir	Good evening
Salut!	Hi!
Ça va?	How are you?
Ça va	Fine

Bonjour, madame

2 Listen as Christine Dachaux, the receptionist at the Hôtel Royal, greets people as they pass through the foyer at lunchtime. How many women does she talk to?

3 It's early evening. Listen to Mme Dachaux again. Which greeting does she use now?

> **En français . . . (In French . . .)**
>
> **Ça va?** is a friendly way of asking how someone is or how things are.
> **Ça va** can be used in a variety of situations to say 'OK' or 'fine'.

4 Two friends, Marc and Julien, meet in the hotel bar. Listen to the way they greet each other and fill the gaps in their conversation.

Julien	.... **Marc. Ça va?**
Marc	.... **Julien.** ....

5 It's 2 p.m. How would you greet:

- the woman sitting in reception?
- M. Dumas who you're meeting for the first time?
- Luc, a good friend?

. . . and goodbye

6 Listen to these key phrases.

Au revoir	Goodbye
Bonsoir	Goodbye
Bonne nuit	Goodnight
et . . . merci!	and . . . thank you!

7 Christine Dachaux is now saying goodbye to some guests. Listen and fill the gaps in the conversation.

Christine	**Au revoir, ...**
Monsieur	**................., madame. Et merci!**
Christine	**Au revoir, ...**
Madame	**Au revoir, madame. ....**

8 Julien and Marc have been joined by some friends. Listen as Julien says goodnight to some of them and tick any names you hear.

Christine ▪   Danièle ▪   Marc ▪   Pierre ▪

9 Now try the following. How would you:

- say good morning to the Hôtel Royal's waiter?
- ask your friend Michèle how she is?
- say thank you to the receptionist as she gives you your key?
- say goodbye to the young woman you have just met in the hotel bar?

> Au revoir, madame

Asking someone's name . . .

1   Listen to these key phrases.

Comment vous appelez-vous?	What's your name?
Et vous?	And you?
Enchanté	Pleased to meet you
Vous êtes . . . ?	Are you . . . ?
Je m'appelle . . .	I am called (my name is) . . .
Non	No
Excusez-moi!	Sorry!

2   There's a wedding reception in the hotel. Listen to a conversation between two people and number these phrases as you hear them.

François Suret.   **Enchanté.**

Comment vous appelez-vous?   **Et vous?**

Je m'appelle Camille Dupuis.

3   Younger guests at the reception use the informal **Comment tu t'appelles?** to ask 'What's your name?' Read their conversation and fill the gaps.

Mélanie	**Comment tu t'appelles?**
Julie	**Julie. Et toi, comment** .... **t'appelles?**
Mélanie	**Je** .... **Mélanie.**

> **En français . . .**
> **vous** and **tu** both mean 'you'. You use:
> **vous** to someone you don't know well and to more than one person;
> **tu** to a close friend, a relative or a child.
> The choice of **vous** or **tu** affects other words:
>
> | | | |
> |---|---|---|
> | **vous** | **Comment vous appelez-vous?** | **Et vous?** |
> | **tu** | **Comment tu t'appelles?** | **Et toi?** |

4   In the foyer, M. Bruno, the hotel manager, is looking for a Mlle Marty. How many women does he talk to?

. . . and introducing yourself

5 Listen to these key phrases.

Je suis . . .	I am . . .
Oui	Yes
Enchantée	Pleased to meet you

> **En français . . .**
> a man says **Enchanté**, a woman says **Enchantée** – spelt differently
> but both sounding the same. Most words which describe (adjectives)
> have a masculine and feminine form, with the feminine (f.) usually
> adding **-e** to the masculine (m.).

6 M. Bruno eventually finds Mlle Marty. Listen as he introduces himself
and fill the gaps below.

M. Bruno	**Mademoiselle Marty?**
Mlle Marty	**Oui, je** .... **Arlette Marty.**
M. Bruno	**Je** .... **Monsieur Bruno. Enchanté,**
	...................**·**
Mlle Marty	.................., **Monsieur Bruno.**

Using the numbers 0 to 10

1 Look at the following handwritten numbers and note how 1 and 7 are
written. Then listen to the numbers 0 to 10 on the audio.

0	1	2	3	4	5	6	7	8	9	10
zéro	un	deux	trois	quatre	cinq	six	sept	huit	neuf	dix

2 Listen and circle the room numbers you hear Christine Dachaux
calling out to the guests: 3   4   5   6   8   1   10

Put it all together

1 Match the English with the French.

a	Thank you	**Ça va?**
b	What's your name?	**Bonsoir!**
c	Are you . . . ?	**Enchanté(e)**
d	I am . . .	**Je suis . . .**
e	Good evening!	**Salut!**
f	Pleased to meet you.	**Comment vous appelez-vous?**
g	How are you?	**Merci**
h	Hi!	**Vous êtes . . . ?**

2 What could these people be saying to each other?

3 Say the following numbers in French, then listen to activity one, page 11, on the audio to check your pronunciation.

5, 10, 3, 7, 6, 9, 2, 4, 8, 1.

4 Can you say the numbers missing from these sequences in French?

- 3, 6, ?
- 0, 5, ?
- 2, 4, ?

"Now you're talking!

1 It's mid-morning and you've arrived at a **gîte** (self-catering accommodation) near La Rochelle. You ring the bell and the landlady opens the door and greets you.

◇ **Ah, bonjour, madame!**
◆ Ask if she is Mme Tubert.
◇ **Oui.**
◆ Greet her and say who you are.
◇ **Enchantée.**
◆ Say you're pleased to meet her.

2 The next day you're on the beach. Mme Tubert's teenage daughter is walking her dog. She greets you.

◇ **Bonjour, madame!**
◆ Say hello and ask her what she's called.
◇ **Virginie. Et vous?**
◆ Say your name.

3 That evening, on your way back to your **gîte**, a neighbour greets you.

◇ **Bonsoir, madame.**
◆ Greet him and introduce yourself.
◇ **Enchanté. Pierre Larrot.**
◆ Say you're pleased to meet him.

4 A week later, you're leaving.

◆ Say goodbye to Mme Tubert and her daughter and thank her.
◇ **Au revoir . . .**

Quiz

1 When can you use **Bonjour**?
2 When talking to a child, should you use **vous** or **tu**?
3 What's the French for 'Pleased to meet you'?
4 Who would you be greeting if you are using **Salut**?
5 At what time of the day do you say **Bonne nuit**?
6 What do you say to apologize if you have made a mistake?
7 What are the two ways of introducing yourself?
8 When asking a child's name do you ask **Comment tu t'appelles?** or **Comment vous appelez-vous?**

Now check whether you can . . .

■ say hello, goodbye and goodnight

■ ask someone how they are

■ say you're fine

■ say thank you

■ introduce yourself

■ ask someone's name

■ apologize if you make a mistake

■ use the numbers 0 to 10

Listen to the audio as often as you can and try to imitate the speakers closely. Saying the words and phrases out loud and repeating them many times will help you to become familiar with the sounds of French and make you more confident.

Vous êtes d'où?

- **giving your nationality**
- **saying where you're from**
- **saying what you do for a living**
- **using the numbers 11 to 20**

En France . . .

there are 22 **régions** (regions) and 96 **départements** (administrative areas). Each **département** has a number which makes up the first two figures of local postcodes and the last two figures of car registration numbers.

As in other countries, you'll hear a wide variety of regional accents. French is also the mother tongue of people in parts of Canada, Belgium and Switzerland, and a second language in North Africa, Egypt, Lebanon, Syria, Cambodia and Vietnam. French Guyana and the islands of La Réunion, Martinique and Guadeloupe are all French-speaking.

Giving your nationality

I   Listen to these key phrases.

Vous êtes anglais/anglaise?   Are you English (m./f.)?
Je suis américain/américaine   I'm American (m./f.)
Je suis français/française   I'm French (m./f.)

En français . . .

a final consonant is not normally pronounced. This means that words
like **français** and **anglais** sound slightly different from the feminine
versions, **française** and **anglaise**, with the added **-e** .

2   Read the following statements and decide which were made by men,
and which by women. Listen to the audio to check your answers.

a **Je suis français**   *b* **Je suis anglaise**
c **Je suis canadien**   *d* **Je suis américain**
e **Je suis anglais**   *f* **Je suis australienne**

3   Match the nationalities to the countries as in the examples, then listen
to some of them on the audio.

anglais(e)   **irlandais(e)**   **américain(e)**   **écossais(e)**   **canadien(ne)**
français(e)   **espagnol(e)**

Pays	Country	Nationalité
Allemagne	*Germany*	allemand(e)
Angleterre	*England*	....
Australie	*Australia*	australien(ne)
Canada	*Canada*	....
Écosse	*Scotland*	....
Espagne	*Spain*	....
États-Unis	*USA*	....
France	*France*	....
Irlande	*Ireland*	....
Pays de Galles	*Wales*	gallois(e)

Saying where you're from

1   Listen to these key phrases.

Vous êtes d'où?   Where are you from?
Vous êtes de . . . ?   Are you from . . . ?
Vous êtes de Londres?   Are you from London?
Je suis de . . .   I'm from . . .

de (from) becomes **d'** before a vowel

2   A group of **étudiants** (students) on a language-learning holiday in Nîmes are asked where they come from by Marie-Pierre, the organiser. Listen and complete their answers.

David   **Je suis de .... , en ....**
Anita   **Je suis de .... , en ....**
Paul   **Je suis de .... , en ....**

En français . . .

the word for 'in' with most countries is **en**:
        en France, en Angleterre, en Australie
. . . but there are exceptions, including:
        au Canada   in Canada
        au pays de Galles   in Wales
        aux États-Unis   in the USA

3   The students are then encouraged to ask questions in French. Listen as Paul asks Marie-Pierre and M. Michaud where they come from and tick the right answer.

| Marie-Pierre | Bordeaux | Bayeux |
| M. Michaud | Nantes | Nîmes |

4   How would you tell a French person where you come from?

Saying what you do for a living

1   Listen to these key phrases.

Quelle est votre profession?	What do you do for a living?
Je suis professeur	I'm a teacher
. . . infirmier/infirmière	. . . a nurse (m./f.)
. . . retraité(e)	. . . retired (m./f.)
Je ne suis pas . . .	I'm not . . .
Je ne travaille pas	I don't work

2   Listen to three people in the group being asked about their work and decide which one is an architect, which one a secretary and which one an engineer. Note that 'a' is not used in French when saying your job title.

a ....

b ....

c ....

architecte
secrétaire
ingénieur

En français . . .

to say that you don't do something, you put the words **ne** and **pas** before and after what you don't do.

      Je <u>ne</u> travaille <u>pas</u>   I don't work

      Je <u>ne</u> comprends <u>pas</u>   I don't understand

3   Of the other three people asked, two don't work and one doesn't understand the question. Listen and fill the gaps in the conversation.

Marie-Pierre	**Paul, quelle est votre profession?**
Paul	**Je ne travaille pas. Je suis ....**
Marie-Pierre	**Et vous, quelle est votre profession?**
David	**Je suis ....**
Marie-Pierre	**Et vous, Marianne, vous êtes .... ?**
Marianne	**Excusez-moi, je ne .... pas.**

Using the numbers 11 to 20

1 Listen to the following numbers, then practise saying them.

| 11 **onze** | 13 **treize** | 15 **quinze** | 17 **dix-sept** | 19 **dix-neuf** |
| 12 **douze** | 14 **quatorze** | 16 **seize** | 18 **dix-huit** | 20 **vingt** |

2 Write in the numbers missing from these sequences:

a **six, dix, ... dix-huit**

b **onze, ... treize**

c **treize, seize, ...**

d **huit, douze, ... vingt**

e **douze, ... dix-huit**

3 Listen to some numbers being read out in random order and underline the ones you hear:

16   11   19   13   20   15   12   14

Which one was not mentioned? What is it in French?

4 Now listen as Marie-Pierre gives the numbers of some French **départements** and write them down under the name.

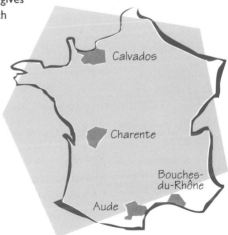

a Calvados

....

b Charente

....

c Aude

....

d Bouches-du-Rhône

....

Put it all together

1 Read this conversation between Marie-Pierre and Barbara and fill the gaps with words from the box.

Marie-Pierre	**Vous êtes** ....?
Barbara	**Non, non. Je suis** ....
Marie-Pierre	**Ah, vous** .... **anglaise!**
	Et vous êtes de Londres?
Barbara	**Non, je** .... **de**
	Chichester.

anglaise

suis

êtes

française

2 How would the following people say where they are from and what their nationality is?

Example: Lina: Madrid, Spain
Je suis de Madrid, en Espagne. Je suis espagnole.

a   Rosie: Sydney, Australia
b   Celia: Manchester, England
c   Andrew: Glasgow, Scotland
d   Philippe: Nice, France
e   Jane: Los Angeles, United States
f   Catherine: Toronto, Canada

3 Can you say these results in French?

France 12	Ireland 15	Wales 11	England 14
Canada 17	USA 16	Australia 20	Germany 19

4 Complete the following in words and figures:

a   **quinze + quatre =** ....   b   **onze + neuf =** ....

c   **seize – trois =** ....   d   **douze + deux =** ....

❝ Now you're talking!

I While in Toulouse, a young woman asks you where **la gare** (the station) is.

◇ **Excusez-moi, monsieur. La gare, s'il vous plaît?**
◆ Say you're not from Toulouse.
◇ **Vous n'êtes pas français?**
◆ Say no, you're English.
◇ **Vous êtes d'où?**
◆ Say you're from Birmingham. Ask her where she's from.
◇ **Je suis de Séville.**
◆ You haven't understood. What do you say?
◇ **Je suis de Séville. Je suis espagnole.**

2 Imagine you're on holiday in France and you get chatting to a woman in the supermarket. Answer her questions with information about yourself.

◇ **Bonjour, madame. Vous êtes américaine?**
◆ You
◇ **Vous êtes d'où?**
◆ You
◇ **Comment vous appelez-vous?**
◆ You

3 A French man you have just met asks you about your work.

◇ **Quelle est votre profession?**
◆ Say you are an engineer. Ask him what he does.
◇ **Je suis professeur.**

Quiz

1   How would you tell someone in French that you're from Bristol?
2   Would a man or a woman say **Je suis française**?
3   What two words would you add to this sentence to say you don't work? **Je** .... **travaille** ....
4   Would you say **Je suis infirmière** if you are a teacher?
5   How many is **quinze**?
6   What do the last two figures on a French car registration plate represent?
7   What would you say to let someone know you don't understand?
8   Which is the odd one out? **Américain**, **Espagne**, **France**.

Now check whether you can . . .

- ■ say what nationality you are
- ■ say where you're from
- ■ say what your occupation is
- ■ ask others for the above information
- ■ say you don't understand
- ■ use the numbers 11 to 20

It is a good idea at this stage to start organising your vocabulary learning. Write new words and phrases in a notebook or on index cards and review them often. Try sticking them on notices on your mirror or kitchen wall or wherever you'll see them regularly. Get friends to test you on vocabulary – they need not be French speakers.

3 TROIS
Voici Émilie

- **introducing friends and family**
- **saying how old you are**
- **talking about your family**
- **using the numbers 21 to 69**

En France . . .

although families are becoming smaller (the average French couple has 1.70 children), people still talk a lot about their children. Don't be surprised to be asked questions about **la famille** (the family) and don't be reserved about asking questions yourself.

Fewer people are getting married in France and 30% of children are born to unmarried parents. You introduce an unmarried partner as **mon ami(e)**.

Introducing friends . . .

1 Listen to these key phrases.

Voici Émilie	This is/Here is Émilie
. . . mon mari	. . . my husband
. . . ma femme	. . . my wife
Voici mes amis	Here are my friends

2 Isabelle Ferri is staying at a campsite near Roscoff. Listen as some neighbours introduce themselves to her and tick the names you hear.

Julien   **Émilie**   **Patrick**   **Marion**   **Nicolas**   **Benoît**

What is Julien's wife called? ....

> **En français . . .**
> there are three words for 'my':
> **mon** for masculine words or before a vowel
> | **mon mari** | my husband |
> |---|---|
> | **mon amie** | my girlfriend/my partner |
> **ma** for feminine words
> | **ma femme** | my wife |
> **mes** for more than one
> | **mes amis** | my friends |

3 Isabelle's husband arrives. Listen and tick:

- what his name is   **Benjamin** ▨   **Luc** ▨
- what nationality he is   **canadien** ▨   **espagnol** ▨

4 Later, by the pool, the Ferris listen to people chatting. Are Catherine and Bernard single, married, divorced or widowed?

	célibataire *(single)*	marié(e) *(married)*	divorcé(e) *(divorced)*	veuf/veuve *(widowed)*
Catherine	▨	▨	▨	▨
Bernard	▨	▨	▨	▨

. . . and family

5 Listen to these key phrases.

Vous avez des enfants?	Do you have any children?
J'ai . . .	I have . . .
. . . une fille	. . . one/a daughter
. . . un fils	. . . one/a son
Je n'ai pas d'enfants	I don't have any children

En français . . .

un means both 'one' and 'a'/'an'. It changes to **une** for the feminine:

<u>un</u> **fils**, <u>une</u> **fille**

des can mean 'some' or 'any':

Vous avez des enfants?	Have you any children?
Il a des enfants	He has some children

But to say 'not any', you use **de/d'**:

Je n'ai pas d'enfants	I don't have any children

---

6 Listen and note how many children Isabelle, Émilie and Marion have.

	fils	fille
Isabelle	1	1
Émilie	0	
Marion	1	2

7 Near them on the campsite is a proud **grand-mère** (grandmother). Read what she says to Isabelle – **a** means 'has'.

Isabelle **Vous avez des enfants?**

Grand-mère **Oui, j'ai une fille, Sabine, et un fils, Luc. Sabine a un fils, Jean-Claude. Luc n'a pas d'enfants.**

Can you say what her daughter's name is, whether she has a son and how many grandchildren she has?

Saying how old you are

1 Listen to these key phrases.

Vous avez quel âge?	How old are you?
Tu as quel âge?	How old are you?
J'ai 20 ans	I am 20

2 Listen and repeat some of the following numbers.

21 vingt et un	**40 quarante**
22 vingt-deux	**41 quarante et un**
23 vingt-trois	**42 quarante-deux**, etc.
24 vingt-quatre	**50 cinquante**
25 vingt-cinq	**51 cinquante et un**
26 vingt-six	**52 cinquante-deux**, etc.
27 vingt-sept	**60 soixante**
28 vingt-huit	**61 soixante et un**
29 vingt-neuf	**62 soixante-deux**, etc.
30 trente	*note that* **et** *is only used to link 20, 30,*
31 trente et un	*40, 50 and 60 with* **un**
32 trente-deux, etc.	

3 Listen and underline any of the following numbers you hear:

25   27   31   33   40   42   51   58   61   67

4 At the seaside, Isabelle hears some young people chatting. Listen and note down their ages.

Aurélien ..21..   Alex ..30..   Elisabeth ..16..

5 M. and Mme Blanc are asked their ages when they enrol for a scubadiving course. Listen and tick the right boxes.

	40	41	45	50	51	55
Mme Blanc	■	■	■	■	■	■
M. Blanc	■	■	■	■	■	■

Talking about your family

1   Listen to these key phrases.

Il/Elle s'appelle comment?   What is his/her name?
Il/Elle s'appelle . . .   He/She's called . . .
Il/Elle a quel âge?   How old is he/she?
Il/Elle a 8 ans   He/She is 8

En français . . .

to talk about age, you use **avoir** (to have).
Il <u>a</u> 8 ans (He's 8) literally means 'He has 8 years'.
Avoir changes depending whether it is with **je**, **tu**, **il/elle**, or **vous**:

     j'<u>ai</u>   I have   **il/elle <u>a</u>**   he/she has
     tu <u>as</u>   you have   **vous <u>avez</u>**   you have

---

2   Isabelle now asks a neighbour at the campsite about her children. Fill the gaps with the words in the box. Then check with the audio.

Isabelle	**Vous .... des enfants?**
Marie-Charlotte	**Oui, j'ai une ....**
Isabelle	**Elle s'appelle comment?**
Marie-Charlotte	**................. s'appelle Valérie.**
Isabelle	**Elle a quel ....?**
Marie-Charlotte	**Elle .... vingt et un ....**

Box:
a
avez
âge
fille
elle
ans

3   Listen to Alain, Catherine and Sabine talking about their families and decide which family belongs to whom.

a ....   *b* ....   *c* ....

Put it all together

1

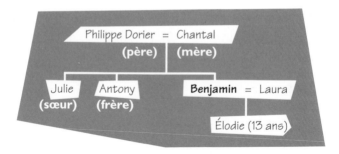

Look at Benjamin's family tree and underline the correct ending for his statements. Can you guess what **est** means?

a	**Ma mère s'appelle**	Philippe, Chantal, Laura
b	**Antony est**	mon frère, mon fils, mon père
c	**Ma fille a**	trois ans, treize ans, trente ans
d	**Julie est**	ma femme, ma mère, ma sœur
e	**Mon père s'appelle**	Antony, Philippe, Benjamin
f	**Laura est**	ma fille, ma femme, ma mère

2 Complete the following statements with **ai**, **as**, **a** or **avez**.

a **Ma fille** _a_ **huit ans.**

b **Vous** _avez_ **un fils?**

c **J'** _ai_ **deux enfants.**

d **Tu** _as_ **quel âge?**

e **Je n'** _ai_ **pas de sœurs.**

3 Look at Martine's family tree and fill the gaps in the following text.

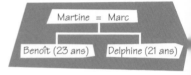

Je .... **Martine.**
Mon .... **s'appelle Marc.**
J'ai un .... **et une** ....
Mon fils a .... **ans. Il s'appelle** ....
Ma fille a .... **Elle** .... **Delphine.**

Now you're talking!

1 Answer the following questions as if you are Sophie Smith, married to Michael, with two children, Anna (12) and Martin (14).

◇ **Bonjour, madame. Comment vous appelez-vous?**
◆ *You*
◇ **Vous êtes mariée?**
◆ *You – introduce your husband*
◇ **Vous avez des enfants?**
◆ *You*
◇ **Et votre fille, elle s'appelle comment?**
◆ *You*
◇ **Elle a quel âge?**
◆ *You*
◇ **Et votre fils, il s'appelle comment?**
◆ *You*
◇ **Il a quel âge?**
◆ *You*

2 You've now started chatting to a woman sitting next to you by the pool.

◆ Ask her if she's married.
◇ **Je suis divorcée.**
◆ Ask her if she has any children.
◇ **Oui, j'ai un fils, Théo.**
◆ Ask her how old Théo is.
◇ **Il a quatorze ans. Ah, voici Théo!**
◆ Say hello to Théo and introduce Martin and Anna to him.

Quiz

1 If you have a daughter, do you have **un fils** or **une fille**?
2 Would you use **mon** or **ma** with **mari**?
3 What is the French for 'single'?
4 How would you say that you don't have any children?
5 When referring to your sister's age, would you say **Il a . . . ans** or **Elle a . . . ans**?
6 To ask a small child how old he or she is, would you say **Tu as quel âge?** or **Vous avez quel âge?**
7 Can you say how old you are in French?
8 If **Henri a cinquante ans**, is he 5, 15 or 50?

Now check whether you can . . .

■ introduce someone – male or female

■ say whether you are married or otherwise

■ say what family you have

■ give your age

■ ask others for the above information

■ ask or say how old someone else is

■ use the numbers 21 to 69

Family photographs provide ideal practice of the language you have learnt in this unit. Point to people and say who they are and what their name is, e.g. **Voici mon fils. Il s'appelle Paul**. You can say how old some of them are – **Louise a 19 ans** – or what they do – **elle est étudiante**. The following words might come in useful:

cousin/cousine	cousin (m./f.)
beau-père, belle-mère	father-in-law, mother-in-law
beau-frère, belle-sœur	brother-in-law, sister-in-law

4

Un thé, s'il vous plaît

- ● ordering a drink in a café
- ● offering, accepting or refusing a drink
- ● asking the price of drinks
- ● using the numbers 70 to 100

En France . . .

to order food and drinks in a café, don't queue at the bar as you would in a pub in the UK, but choose a table and wait to be served.

If the waiter/waitress is a bit slow in coming, you can get his/her attention by saying: **Monsieur, s'il vous plaît!** or **Madame, s'il vous plaît!**

Prices in cafés vary a lot depending on the popularity of the place. You'll also pay more if you sit outside.

Ordering a drink . . .

1   Listen to these key phrases.

Vous désirez?	What would you like?
Un thé, s'il vous plaît	A tea, please
. . . au lait	. . . with milk
. . . au citron	. . . with lemon
Pour moi, un café	For me, a coffee
Voilà!	Here you are!
Très bien	Very well
Alors	Then, well then/Right!

2   Listen to Pierre and Nathalie ordering teas in a café. Do they order tea with milk or with lemon, or do they order **thé nature** (black tea)?

Nathalie   ....
Pierre   ....

En français . . .

all nouns (not just those referring to people) are either masculine or feminine and this affects the words for 'a' and 'the'.
The words for 'a' are **un** (m.) and **une** (f.) and it is a good idea to learn new words together with **un** or **une**.

un café	a coffee	**un jus de fruits**	a fruit juice
un vin rouge	a red wine	**un jus d'orange**	an orange juice
un vin blanc	a white wine	**un coca**	a coke
une limonade	a lemonade	**une pression**	a draught beer
une bière	a beer	**une eau minérale**	a mineral water

3   Four friends join Pierre and Nathalie. Listen to the drinks being ordered and tick the ones you hear on the list above.

. . . in a café

4 Jean, the waiter, is confirming some drinks orders.
Has he got them right? Listen out for **bouteilles** (bottles).

  a **un coca, une limonade, un Orangina**
  b **un café, une pression et deux Schweppes**
  c **deux bouteilles de champagne**
  d **un vin blanc et une eau minérale**

En français . . .

as in English, nouns usually add **-s** when there are more than one but
in French you don't hear it:

> **Une bouteille de champagne, s'il vous plaît.**
> **Deux bouteilles de champagne, s'il vous plaît.**

---

5 Listen to Pierre and Nathalie ordering coffees for their friends. Refer
to the **En France . . .** box below and fill the gaps.

Jean	**Vous .... ?**
Nathalie	**Deux cafés, un .... café et un ....**
	crème.
Jean	**Alors deux .... , un .... et un**
	.... crème.

En France . . .

coffee is very strong and therefore served in small quantities. If you
order **un café**, you'll get an expresso. If you want a bigger coffee, ask
for **un grand café** (a large coffee). If you want a white coffee, ask
for **un café au lait** or **un café crème**.

Offering, accepting or refusing a drink

I   Listen to these key phrases.

Qu'est-ce que vous désirez?	What would you like?
Vous voulez un apéritif?	Do you want an aperitif?
D'accord	OK/Agreed
Oui, merci	Yes, please
Non, merci	No, thank you
À votre santé!	Cheers!

2   Michel is offering his new neighbours, M. and Mme Blois, an aperitif.
Mme Blois only wants **un verre d'eau** (a glass of water). Listen and
fill the gaps below.

Michel	**Vous .... un apéritif, Madame Blois?**
Mme Blois	**Non, merci. Pour ...., un verre d'eau.**
Michel	**Et vous, Monsieur Blois? Un apéritif?**
M. Blois	**Oui, ...**
Michel	**Qu'est-ce que vous ....? Un martini, un porto, un whisky?**
M. Blois	**Un porto, s'il vous plaît.**
Michel	**D'accord. .... À votre santé!**

À votre santé!

Can you guess what **un porto** is?

En français . . .

there are various ways of asking the same question. To ask 'What
would you like?' you can either use **Qu'est-ce que . . . ?** (What . . . ?):
   Qu'est-ce que vous désirez?

or simply make the statement **Vous désirez** sound like a question by
raising your intonation at the end.
   Vous désirez?

Asking the price of drinks

1 Listen to these key phrases.

C'est combien?	How much is it?
Ça fait . . .	That'll be . . .
Un euro, soixante-dix	1 euro, 70 centimes

2 Listen to some of these numbers between 70 and 100.

70	**soixante-dix**	80	**quatre-vingts**
71	**soixante et onze**	81	**quatre-vingt-un**
72	**soixante-douze**	82	**quatre-vingt-deux**, etc.
73	**soixante-treize**	90	**quatre-vingt-dix**
74	**soixante-quatorze**	91	**quatre-vingt-onze**
75	**soixante-quinze**	92	**quatre-vingt-douze**
76	**soixante-seize**	93	**quatre-vingt-treize**
77	**soixante-dix-sept**	94	**quatre-vingt-quatorze**, etc.
78	**soixante-dix-huit**	99	**quatre-vingt-dix-neuf**
79	**soixante-dix-neuf**	100	**cent**

3 Now listen as Pierre and Nathalie check prices in their local bar. Tick the price you hear.

Une bouteille de vin	13,80 € ■	13,85 € ■	13,90 € ■
Un verre de champagne	7,70 € ■	7,75 € ■	7,77 € ■
Deux martinis	9,24 € ■	9,48 € ■	9,80 € ■

4 Jean is adding up three orders. Listen and write down the totals.

a ....   *b* ....   *c* ....

En France . . .

the currency is the **euro**, written as €. There are 100 **cents** or **centimes** in one **euro**. 10,50 € = **dix euros, cinquante (cents)**; 100 € = **cent euros**; 200 € = **deux cents euros**.

Put it all together

1 You want to order the following drinks. Would you use **un** or **une**? Fill the gaps.

a .... **café**   *b* .... **bière**   *c* .... **thé**

d .... **limonade**   *e* .... **coca**   *f* .... **Orangina**

g .... **eau minérale** *h* .... **jus de fruits**

2 Match up the questions and answers:

a **Qu'est-ce que vous désirez?**   **Une limonade, s'il vous plaît.**

b **C'est combien?**   **Oui, un jus d'orange.**

c **Vous désirez un thé au lait?**   **Ça fait douze euros.**

d **Vous voulez un jus de fruits?**   **Non, un thé au citron.**

e **Vous voulez un apéritif?**   **Oui, un martini, s'il vous plaît.**

3 Complete this conversation with the words from the box:

Jean	**Vous** ....?
Nathalie	**Un thé,** ....
Jean	**Nature, lait,** ....?
Nathalie	**Au lait.**
Jean	.................!
Nathalie	**C'est** ....?
Jean	**Un euro, soixante.**
Nathalie	**Voilà.** ....

> Voilà
> Merci
> combien
> désirez
> citron
> s'il vous plaît

4 Complete the following in words and figures:

a **quarante-cinq + sept =** ....

b **soixante et onze + neuf =** ....

c **cinquante-trois + vingt =** ....

d **quatre-vingt-quinze – cinq =** ....

Now you're talking!

1 Imagine you're sitting in a café in Nantes.

> ◆ Call the waiter over.
> ◇ **Bonjour, messieurs dames. Vous désirez?**
> ◆ Order one large coffee, a tea and an orange juice.
> ◇ **Très bien. Merci.**
> ◆ When the drinks arrive, thank the waiter and ask how much it comes to.
> ◇ **Ça fait 5,20 €.**
> ◆ Give him the money and say 'here you are'.

2 Now imagine you're having a drink in a smart café in Paris. The waitress greets you.

> ◇ **Madame, monsieur, bonjour. Vous désirez?**
> ◆ Order a coke and a beer.
> ◇ **Bouteille? Pression?**
> ◆ Order a draught beer.
> ◇ **Très bien.**
> ◆ When the drinks arrive, ask the price.
> ◇ **Ça fait 10,70 €.**

3 It's your birthday. **Joyeux anniversaire!** Happy birthday! How would you order a bottle of champagne?

4 Your French neighbours on the campsite have come for a chat.

> ◆ Ask them if they want an aperitif.
> ◇ **Oui, merci.**
> ◆ Ask them what they'd like. A martini or a whisky?
> ◇ **Pour moi, un martini.**
> ◇ **Un whisky pour moi, s'il vous plaît.**
> ◆ Give them their drinks and say 'Cheers!'

Quiz

1   Which is the odd one out: **eau**, **champagne**, **bière**?
2   Do you order **un grand café** or **un café crème** if you want a white coffee?
3   Name three drinks beginning with 'c' in French.
4   Is **quatre-vingt-dix** 70 or 90?
5   If you want draught beer do you ask for **bouteille** or **pression**?
6   How do you say 'Cheers' in French?
7   Which is the most expensive part of a café to drink in?
8   What does **C'est combien?** mean?
9   How would you accept if someone offered you a drink?

Now check whether you can . . .

◼ order a drink in a bar

◼ offer someone a drink

◼ accept when someone offers you a drink

  . . . or refuse politely

◼ say 'Cheers'

◼ ask the price of drinks

◼ understand and use the numbers 70 to 100

Make your French learning relevant to *you* and part of your everyday life. When you have a drink, think of the word in French; when buying a round of drinks, try to memorise the list in French. If you have a dictionary, you can increase your vocabulary by looking up any drinks you, your friends and family enjoy.

Contrôle 1

1. Choose the right phrase for each situation.

   a saying 'Cheers'
   b you're off to bed
   c handing someone a drink
   d you don't understand
   e you're introduced to someone
   f you want to apologise
   g you ask someone how they are

2. Listen to Mme Chevalier checking in at the hotel and complete her details on the form below. Note how French people give their phone numbers two digits at a time.

Nom	Chevalier
Prénom	
Adresse	avenue de la Gare
	30100 Alès
Numéro de téléphone	04 98 35

Can you say your home and work telephone numbers in French?

3 Listen to students from the Nîmes language school introducing
themselves. Choose the right nationality from the list and complete
the table. Also, correct any mistakes which have crept into the table.

anglais	anglaise
allemand	allemande
espagnol	espagnole
canadien	canadienne

Nom	Nationalité	Domicile *(Home)*
Rosanna	....	Barcelone
Wilfried	....	Munich
Elisabeth	....	Stirling, Écosse
Nicole	....	New York
Paul	....	Londres

4 Listen as Jean, the waiter, reads out some prices from the menu.
Number the prices you hear in the order you hear them.

14,50 €	7,30 €	8,75 €	20,45 €	17,75 €	6,90 €
....	....	....	....	....	....

5 Practise pronouncing
the names of these French
towns, then check
your pronunciation
with the audio.
Note that 'h' is silent
in French and that the final 's'
is not spoken in any of these
names, as with most French
words ending in 's'.

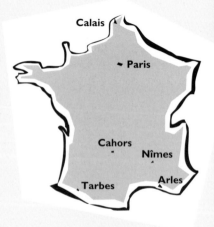

Calais

Paris

Cahors

Nîmes

Tarbes

Arles

6   Imagine you're in a French café. The waiter comes over.

◇ **Bonjour, ... Vous désirez?**
◆ Order one white tea, one beer and one glass of water.
◇ **Très bien . . . la bière: pression ou bouteille?**
◆ Ask for a bottle.

The waiter brings the drinks and says:
◇ **Vous êtes américain(e)?**
◆ Say no, English.
◇ **Vous êtes d'où ?**
◆ Say you are from Bristol.

◆ Later on, ask how much it is.
◇ **Ça fait 10,70 €.**
◆ Give the money and say thank you.

7   Draw your family tree with parents, brothers and sisters and your children if you have any. Imagine you are introducing each member to a French acquaintance. Can you say who they are and how old they are?

8   A neighbour asks for your help when her daughter receives a letter in French from a Swiss penfriend. Translate the first page of the letter for them. Some extra vocabulary is given on the right.

Chère Anna,
Je m'appelle Julie. Je suis de Genève, en Suisse. J'ai 14 ans.

J'ai un frère et une sœur. Ma sœur a 18 ans, elle est fille au pair en Allemagne. Mon frère a 23 ans. Il est en France. Il est marié mais il n'a pas d'enfants.

Mon père est architecte et ma mère est professeur de français.

cher/chère dear
Suisse Switzerland
professeur de français
French teacher

1 Can you find six drinks in this **mots cachés** (word puzzle)?

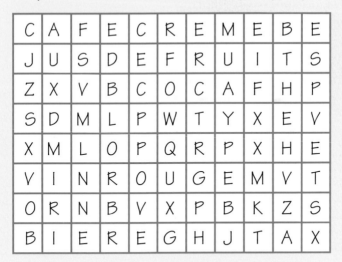

C	A	F	E	C	R	E	M	E	B	E
J	U	S	D	E	F	R	U	I	T	S
Z	X	V	B	C	O	C	A	F	H	P
S	D	M	L	P	W	T	Y	X	E	V
X	M	L	O	P	Q	R	P	X	H	E
V	I	N	R	O	U	G	E	M	V	T
O	R	N	B	V	X	P	B	K	Z	S
B	I	E	R	E	G	H	J	T	A	X

Learning a new language often involves guessing the meaning of words. Many French and English words have the same root, so you can guess with confidence. However, remember that while words may look the same or similar, they generally sound quite different – you've already met some of these – **six**, **orange**, **fruits**, **architecte** and **Irlande**.

5

Où est la poste?

- **asking where something is**
- **. . . and how far it is**
- **saying where you live and work**

En France . . .

most towns have by-passes. If you're driving and wish to visit the centre of a town, look out for the sign **CENTRE-VILLE**. Otherwise follow the sign **TOUTES DIRECTIONS** (all directions).

The railway station (**la gare**) is often indicated by the abbreviation **SNCF**.

If you need to declare the loss or theft of any belongings, go to the police station (called **gendarmerie** in the country and **commissariat** in a town) or the **mairie** (town hall).

Asking where something is . . .

1   Listen to these key phrases.

Pardon . . .	Excuse me . . .
Où est la poste?	Where is the post office?
Où sont les magasins?	Where are the shops?
C'est ici/là	It's here/there
Le cinéma est en face de la gare	The cinema is opposite the station
La gare est près de l'église	The station is near the church

2   Pierre asks Virginie to point out some local landmarks on his map. First check the meanings of the words in the glossary.

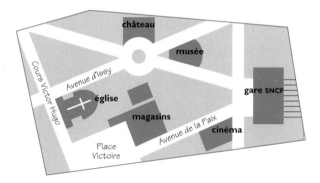

Now listen and match the buildings with the phrases below.

a   **c'est ici**   *b*   **est en face de la gare**
c   **est là**   *d*   **sont près de l'église**

En français . . .

the words for 'the' are . . .

le	m.	**le château, le magasin**
la	f.	**la banque** (bank), **la poste**
les	plural m./f.	**les magasins, les églises**

le and **la** become **l'** before a vowel or **h**   **l'hôtel, l'église**

. . . and how far it is

3 Listen to these key phrases.

C'est loin?	Is it far?
C'est à dix minutes	It's ten minutes away
C'est à cent mètres	It's a hundred metres away
C'est à cinq cents mètres	It's five hundred metres
. . . de la gare	. . . from the station

4 Listen to some tourists enquiring how far **la plage** (the beach), **le marché** (the market) and the town centre are. Note down what they're told.

	la plage	le marché	le centre-ville
distance	....	....	....

5 Now listen as they enquire about some other places and fill the gaps.

a .... **est à côté du café.**

b .... **est avant la gare.**

c .... **est en face de l'église.**

d .... **est après le château.**

e **C'est à trois** .... **mètres de la banque.**

> **à côté de** next to
> **avant** before
> **après** after
> **en face de** opposite

En français . . .

de and **le** combine and become **du:**

    en face du château

    à côté du café

Saying where you live . . .

1 Listen to these key phrases.

Vous habitez où?	Where do you live?
J'habite . . .	I live . . .
Il/Elle habite . . .	He/She lives . . .
. . . en ville	. . . in town
. . . à la campagne	. . . in the countryside
. . . dans un petit village	. . . in a small village

2 Bernard asks three people he has just met where they live. Listen and tick the right box.

	en ville	à la campagne	dans un petit village
1	▬	▬	▬
2	▬	▬	▬
3	▬	▬	▬

3 Later, one of his colleagues asks him where he lives, using the informal **tu habites**. Listen to discover whether he lives in town or not.

En français . . .

the ending of a verb e.g. **habiter** (to live), **travailler** (to work), changes if it is with **je**, **tu**, **il/elle**, **nous** (we), **vous** or **ils/elles** (they).

		travailler	habiter
I	**je/j'**	travaille	habite
you (informal)	**tu**	travaille**s**	habite**s**
he/she	**il/elle**	travaille	habite
we	**nous**	travaill**ons**	habit**ons**
you	**vous**	travaill**ez**	habit**ez**
they	**ils/elles**	travaill**ent**	habit**ent**

All except the **nous** and **vous** forms sound exactly the same. A large group of French verbs end in **-er** and follow this pattern.

. . . and work

4 Listen to these key phrases.

Vous travaillez où?	Where do you work?
Je travaille . . . à Paris	I work . . . in Paris
Il/Elle travaille . . .	He/She works . . .
. . . dans un bureau	. . . in an office
. . . chez Peugeot	. . . at Peugeot
. . . chez moi	. . . at home
. . . pour une compagnie américaine	. . . for an American company

5 Listen to Bernard talking about himself and his family and finish the sentences with one of the key phrases.

Mon frère travaille ....•
Ma sœur travaille ....• **Elle travaille** ....
...................• **Et ma femme travaille** ....•
Moi, je travaille chez moi.

Where does Bernard work?

> **En français . . .**
>
> **chez X** means 'at the house/home/place/company of X'.
>
> **Chez mon frère.** At my brother's house.

6 Now listen to some people who do not work. Tick the reason why.

	mère de famille (housewife)	au chômage (unemployed)	retraité(e) (retired)	étudiant(e) (student)
a				
b				
c				
d				

Put it all together

1   If you were looking for the places listed
    below which signs would you follow?

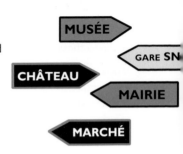

   a   station
   b   museum
   c   castle
   d   market

2   The grid below shows the distance between a few northern towns
    and Dunkerque. Practise reading them aloud. For example, **Calais est
    à quarante-deux kilomètres**.

Calais	Lille	Boulogne	Le Touquet	Montreuil
42 km	77 km	80 km	95 km	98 km

3   Do you know the correct form of 'the' to use – **le**, **la**, **l'** or **les** for
    each of these places?

   a .... **musée**   *b* .... **hôtel**
   c .... **gare**   *d* .... **restaurant**
   e .... **cinéma**   *f* .... **poste**

4   Read these statements and say whether they are **vrai** (true) or **faux**
    (false) for you and your town.

   a **La banque est en face de la poste.**
   b **Le musée est à côté de l'église.**
   c **J'habite près du cinéma.**
   d **Je travaille dans un bureau à cent mètres de la gare.**

Now you're talking!

1 Imagine you're in the **office du tourisme** (tourist office) and the clerk is showing you the map of the town.

- ◆ Ask him where the hotel is.
- ◇ **C'est là.**
- ◆ Now ask where the castle is.
- ◇ **Le château, c'est là, en face de la mairie.**
- ◆ Ask if it's far.
- ◇ **Non, c'est à cinq minutes d'ici.** (from here)
- ◆ Ask where the museum and the church are.
- ◇ **Alors, le musée est ici et l'église est là.**

2 It's the afternoon and you're now in a café.

- ◆ Call the waitress and order a white coffee.
- ◇ **Bien, madame.**
- ◆ Ask her where the bank is.
- ◇ **C'est là, à cent mètres du café.**

Later on you start chatting to her.

- ◆ Ask her if she lives in town.
- ◇ **Non, j'habite dans un petit village à la campagne.**
- ◆ Ask if it's far.
- ◇ **Non, c'est à vingt kilomètres.**

3 Now she asks you a few questions. Can you tell her:

- ◆ what nationality you are?
- ◆ where you are from?
- ◆ where you live – town, countryside or small village?
- ◆ what your job is?
- ◆ where you work?

Quiz

1 What do **le** and **la** both mean?
2 If someone works **dans un bureau,** where do they work?
3 **Avant** is the opposite of ....
4 Does **à côté de** mean 'next to' or 'opposite'?
5 If you're looking for the station, do you ask for **la gare** or **la poste**?
6 If **cinq cents mètres** is 500 metres then what do you think the French for 400 metres would be?
7 How would you say 'It's 10 minutes away' in French?
8 Is the French for 'shop': **château**, **magasin** or **musée**?

Now check whether you can . . .

■ ask where a specific place in town is

■ ask if it's far

■ understand basic town signs

■ ask others where they live and work

■ give this information about yourself

Learning the patterns of French (i.e. the grammar) allows you to say what you want to say without relying on set phrases.

Parler is the French for 'speak' and it follows exactly the same pattern as **habiter** and **travailler**. So, to say what languages you speak, you say for example **Je parle anglais, je ne parle pas allemand**. To ask if someone speaks English, you say **Vous parlez anglais?** (The French words for languages are the same as the masculine nationalities on page 16.)

SIX

Il y a une piscine ici?

- asking for a specific place
  - . . . and making simple enquiries
- understanding basic directions
- asking for help to understand

En France . . .

when you're reading a French road map, bear in mind that **A** indicates an **autoroute** or motorway; **N** indicates a **route nationale** or main road which is usually very busy; **D** a **route départementale** or small road – normally very pleasant to drive on as long as you're not in too much of a hurry!

Most motorways are signposted in blue and are toll roads (**autoroutes à péage**). If you drive a long distance, you'll have to pay several times because sections of motorway belong to different companies. You can pay by credit card.

Asking for a specific place . . .

1   Listen to these key phrases.

Il y a une piscine ici	There is a swimming pool here
Il y a des magasins	There are some shops
Il y a un supermarché ici?	Is there a supermarket here?
Il y en a trois	There are three
Il n'y a pas de . . . ici	There aren't any . . . here

En français . . .

il y a means 'there is' and 'there are'. You add **en** (of them) when specifying a number:

    Il y en a deux. There are two <u>of them</u>.

'There is *not*/There are *not*' is **il n'y a pas de . . .**

    Il n'y a pas de restaurant ici.

2   Listen to people enquiring about local amenities in Boulogne. Some you have already met, some you will be able to guess or look up in the glossary. Link each one with its location.

la rue street
la place square

a	**des taxis**	**rue de la Gare**
b	**un supermarché**	**place du Marché**
c	**une piscine**	**centre-ville**
d	**des magasins**	**place de la République**
e	**un camping**	**centre-ville**
f	**un parking**	**rue de Paris**

3   How would you ask if there is one of the following?

- campsite
- post office
- swimming pool
- bank

. . . and making simple enquiries

4 Listen to the key phrase.

Est-ce qu'il y a . . .   Is there . . .
   un garage   a garage
   près d'ici?   near here?

5 Caroline's **voiture** (car) has broken down. Listen to the audio and read the dialogue below. Then find the French for . . .

a my car has broken down
b a phone box
c over there

Caroline	**Excusez-moi, monsieur. Ma voiture est en panne. Est-ce qu'il y a un garage près d'ici?**
Monsieur	**À douze kilomètres, madame.**
Caroline	**Oh, c'est loin! Il y a une cabine téléphonique près d'ici?**
Monsieur	**Oui, il y en a une là-bas.**

6 Now listen to four tourists making enquiries. Is the map correct?

Change it if necessary.

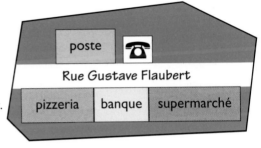

Understanding basic directions . . .

I Listen to these key phrases.

Pour aller à . . . ?	To get to . . . ?
Allez tout droit	Go straight on
Continuez tout droit	Carry straight on
Tournez à droite	Turn right
Tournez à gauche	Turn left
Prenez . . .	Take . . .
. . . la première à droite	. . . the first on the right
puis . . .	then . . .
. . . la deuxième à gauche	. . . the second on the left

2 Listen to Caroline making some more enquiries. Which letters on the map correspond to the following three places?

- **l'office du tourisme**

- **le marché**

- **l'hôpital** (hospital)

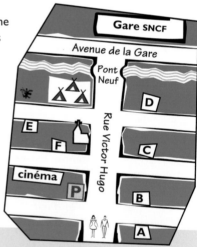

En français . . .

you'll notice that the ordinal numbers (second, third, fourth, etc.) all end in **-ième** – **deuxième**, **troisième**, **quatrième**, etc. The one important exception is 'first', which is **premier/première** (m./f.).

3 Caroline now enquires about the station, the cinema and the campsite. Listen and look carefully at the map above. Are these three places correctly marked on the map?

. . . and asking for help to understand

4   Listen to these key phrases.

Vous pouvez . . .   Can you . . .
. . . répéter, s'il vous plaît?   . . . repeat, please?
. . . parler plus lentement?   . . . speak more slowly?

5   Two English tourists find it difficult to understand the directions they are given. Can you help them? Listen to the audio and note down which way they should be going.

Peter   ....

Anna   ....

6   Peter is now looking for a swimming pool. Listen and fill the gaps in the dialogue below.

Peter	**Il y a une .... ici?**
Dame	**Oui, place de la République. Prenez la .... à droite, puis tournez à ....**
Peter	**Vous pouvez .... , s'il vous plaît?**
Dame	**Oui, ... la deuxième à droite, puis tournez à gauche. C'est .... de la République.**
Peter	**Merci, madame.**

7   Anna isn't sure how to get back to the station to catch her train home. Listen and note down the route she should take.

....

8   How would you ask:

- if there's a bank near here?
- if there's a campsite near the station?
- someone to repeat what they said?

Put it all together

1 Complete each gap in the text with one word from the box.

* .... aller à l'Hôtel du Golf, s'il vous plaît?
* **Continuez tout** ...., ... à **gauche puis prenez la** .... à **droite, juste en** .... **de la poste.**
* **Vous pouvez parler plus** ...., **s'il vous plaît?**

> pour
> face
> deuxième
> lentement
> droit
> tournez

2 You are now looking for the swimming pool. A passer-by gives you some directions.

La piscine? Allez tout droit, prenez la troisième à gauche et c'est à droite, après le camping.

Now look again at the map on page 54 and see if you can mark the position of the swimming pool.

3 Using **il y a** and **il n'y a pas de**, can you say what there is and what there isn't in your home town?

4 Can you make the connection? Match a word from each column.

a	**piscine**	**autoroute**
b	**gauche**	**banque**
c	**hôpital**	**eau**
d	**panne**	**infirmière**
e	**franc**	**droite**
f	**à péage**	**garage**

Now you're talking!

I Imagine you are in Villeneuve for the first time and need some help to find your way around.

◆ Stop a female passer-by politely and ask if there's a tourist office here.

◇ **Prenez la deuxième à droite, puis la première à gauche.**

◆ Ask whether it's far.

◇ **Non, c'est à dix minutes.**

◆ Ask whether there's a post office nearby.

◇ **Oui, il y en a une après la place du marché, à gauche.**

◆ You didn't quite catch the last bit – ask her to repeat that.

◇ **La poste est après la place du marché, à gauche.**

◆ Thank her and say goodbye.

2 You've now found the tourist office.

◆ Ask the man behind the desk if there's a bank near here.

◇ **Il y en a trois. Il y en a une place du Marché.**

◆ You don't understand. Ask him to speak more slowly.

◇ **Il y a une banque place du Marché. Continuez tout droit et prenez la deuxième rue à gauche.**

◆ Ask him if it's far.

◇ **Oh, non, c'est à cinq minutes.**

◆ Ask him if there's a cinema here.

◇ **Non, il n'y a pas de cinéma ici.**

◆ Thank him and say goodbye.

3 Later, you're walking in the town centre when another tourist stops you for directions.

◇ **Pardon. Il y a une banque près d'ici?**

◆ Say the bank is over there, on the right.

◇ **Là-bas, à droite? C'est loin?**

◆ Say, no, it's two minutes away.

Quiz

1   How do you say 'there is' or 'there are'?
2   Where do you go if your car is **en panne**?
3   What does the sign **PÉAGE** on the motorway mean?
4   If you want a quiet drive should you choose a **route départementale** or a **route nationale**?
5   Fill the gap: **première**, ..., **troisième**.
6   If you want a swim do you look for the sign **PLACE**, **PARC** or **PISCINE**?
7   What word do you need to add to **il y** .... **a trois** to mean 'there are three of them?'
8   True or false? **Vous pouvez parler plus lentement?** means 'Could you repeat that, please?'

Now check whether you can . . .

■   ask if there is a specific place in town

■   make simple enquiries

■   ask how to get to a specific place

■   understand basic directions

■   ask someone to repeat something or talk slowly

■   say 'first', 'second', etc. in French

The best way to make progress is to speak French as often as you can. Keep it very simple and don't worry about mistakes at this stage – you will learn more by practising than by waiting until you are word perfect. Don't hesitate to ask people to repeat what they have said or to speak more slowly.

Je voudrais une chambre

- saying which type of room you want
  . . . and how long you want it for
- spelling your name
- booking a room and paying for it

En France . . .

you'll find that hotels are often cheaper than their British equivalents. They charge per room rather than per person, but breakfast is usually extra. If you see the sign **COMPLET**, it means the hotel is full.

You won't often find Bed & Breakfasts in towns, but when driving through the countryside you'll see them indicated by the occasional **CHAMBRES D'HÔTES** sign.

Hotels and campsites are usually well signposted, but don't be misled by the sign **HÔTEL DE VILLE** – this indicates the town hall and not a hotel!

Saying which type of room you want . . .

1 Listen to these key phrases.

Je voudrais une chambre . . .   I would like a room . . .
. . . pour une personne   . . . for one person
. . . pour deux personnes   . . . for two people
au premier (1ᵉʳ) étage   on the first floor
avec . . .   with . . .
. . . salle de bains   . . . bathroom
. . . douche   . . . shower
. . . WC   . . . toilet

2 Listen to Nicolas enquiring about a single room in the Hôtel Royal. Does he choose one with a shower or a bathroom?

3 As Nicolas waits in reception he listens to someone asking for a double room. Does he want it . . .

a  **avec deux lits?**

b **avec un grand lit?**

4 Listen to two more people choosing their rooms. Tick the floor they choose.

	1ᵉʳ étage	2ᵉ étage	3ᵉ étage	4ᵉ étage
a				
b				

(**deuxième**, **troisième**, etc. are often abbreviated to 2ᵉ, 3ᵉ, etc.)

5 How would you ask for these rooms?

. . . and how long you want it for

6 Listen to these key phrases.

Pour combien de nuits?	For how many nights?
Pour . . . une nuit	For . . . one night
. . . trois nuits	. . . three nights
. . . une semaine	. . . one week
. . . ce soir	. . . tonight
. . . demain	. . . tomorrow

7 The Hôtel Royal is busy. Listen to four people asking about a room and note down how long they wish to stay. Listen out for **seulement**, which means 'only'.

a ....   b ....

c ....   d ....

8 If you book into a hotel in France the receptionist may ask you to spell your name – **Vous pouvez épeler?** Listen to the alphabet in French and make sure you know how to spell out your name.

A B C D E F G H I J K L M N O P Q R S T U V W X Y Z

9 Listen to more of Nicolas's conversation with the receptionist. His **prénom** (first name) is Nicolas – can you work out what his **nom** (surname) is?

10 Now practise spelling the names of your friends and relations.

Booking a room . . .

1   Listen to these key phrases.

Je voudrais réserver une chambre   I'd like to book a room
. . . pour le premier septembre   . . . for September 1st
. . . du 2 au 5 mai   . . . from 2nd until 5th May

janvier	January	**juillet**	July
février	February	**août**	August
mars	March	**septembre**	September
avril	April	**octobre**	October
mai	May	**novembre**	November
juin	June	**décembre**	December

En français . . .

for dates, you use **premier** for the first of the month and cardinal
numbers (**deux**, **trois**, **quatre**, etc.) for the other days.

le premier juillet   the first of July
le quatorze avril   the fourteenth of April

2   Listen to four people talking about their bookings and note down their
    dates.

a **Pour** ....   *b* **du** .... **au** .... **juin**
c **Pour** ....   *d* **du** .... **au** .... **août**

3   Now it's your turn. Say you'd like to book a room – **Je voudrais
    réserver une chambre** – for the following dates:

a 15/7   *b* 10/4   *c* 1/8   *d* 3–6/9   *e* 11–14/5   *f* 1–4/6

. . . and paying for it

4 Listen to these key phrases.

Le petit déjeuner est compris?	Is breakfast included?
Non, il est en supplément	No, it's extra
Je peux payer . . .	Can I pay . . .
. . . avec une carte de crédit?	. . . by credit card?

5 Listen to Marie enquiring about rooms in the Hôtel Royal. Do they cost **cent quinze euros**, **cent cinquante euros** or **deux cents euros**? Tick the right price.

Price of rooms   **115** € ■   **150** € ■   **200** € ■

> **En français . . .**
>
> **cent** (hundred) adds an **-s** only when the number is in round hundreds:
>> **deux cents** (200), **cinq cents** (500)
>
> but . . .
>> **deux cent cinquante** (250), **cinq cent un** (501)

6 Now listen to the last conversation again. Will the hotel accept payment by credit card? How much extra is breakfast **par personne** (per person)?

Petit déjeuner   **7** € ■   **8** € ■   **18** € ■

7 How would you:
- say you'd like to book a double room with bath for a week?
- ask how much it is?
- ask if breakfast is included?
- ask if you can pay by credit card?

Put it all together

1 Find the right ending for the following:

a	**Je voudrais une chambre pour . . .**	premier étage
b	**Je voudrais une chambre avec . . .**	semaine
c	**C'est pour une . . .**	en supplément
d	**Je peux payer avec . . . ?**	deux personnes
e	**Le petit déjeuner est . . . ?**	épeler, s'il vous plaît
f	**C'est 8 euros . . .**	compris
g	**La chambre est au . . .**	deux lits
h	**Vous pouvez . . . ?**	une carte de crédit

2 Now how would you ask . . .

a for a double room for a week?
b for a single room for three nights?
c if breakfast is included?
d for a room on the second floor?

3 If you asked the proprietors of the Hôtel du Château the following questions, would they answer **oui** or **non**?

a **Le petit déjeuner est en supplément?**
b **Il y a un parking?**
c **C'est loin, le centre-ville?**
d **Il y a une piscine?**

Hôtel du Château
Alvignac, Tél. 05.65.33.60.14

- **35 chambres avec s.d.b., TV**
- **Prix des chambres: 35 / 75 €**
- **Petit déjeuner: 6 €**
- **Parking privé**
- **À 500 m du centre-ville**

" Now you're talking!

I   Imagine you're driving down to Cannes with a friend and you need to find a room for tonight. You've found a hotel you like the look of.

◆ Greet the male receptionist and say you'd like a room for tonight.
◇ **Oui, madame. Qu'est-ce que vous désirez?**
◆ Say you'd like a double room.
◇ **Très bien. Avec un grand lit ou avec deux lits?**
◆ Say you'd like a room with twin beds.
◇ **Bien. Avec salle de bains ou avec douche?**
◆ Say with bathroom, and ask how much it is.
◇ **Une chambre pour deux personnes avec salle de bains, ça fait 60 €.**
◆ Ask whether breakfast is included.
◇ **Non, il est en supplément.**
◆ Ask how much it is.
◇ **Ça fait 6,50 € par personne.**

2   You enjoyed your stay so much that you decide to use the hotel for your return trip.

◆ Say you'd like to book a room for 22nd July. This time you'd like a room with twin beds and a shower.
◇ **Oui, madame.**
◆ Ask if you can pay by credit card.
◇ **Oui, madame.**
◆ Ask how much it is.
◇ **Ça fait 53 €, madame.**

Quiz

1 Would you be able to get breakfast at a **hôtel de ville**?
2 When do hotels put up the sign **COMPLET**?
3 If you want a shower in your room do you ask for a **salle de bains** or a **douche**?
4 If your room is on the fourth floor, is it **au cinquième étage** or **au quatrième étage**?
5 Name three months which begin with 'j' in French.
6 How do you spell in French the name **Dupuis**?
7 True or false: you could go for a swim before breakfast if the hotel has a **piscine**?
8 Is a week **un soir**, **une nuit** or **une semaine**?

Now check whether you can . . .

■ ask for a single or double room

■ specify what kind of double room you want

■ say what washing facilities you want

■ say how long you wish to stay

■ understand which floor your room is on

■ say you'd like to book a room

■ spell out your name

Before you listen to, or take part in, a conversation, picture yourself in that particular situation. What would you say and hear if you were in a hotel in your own country, for example? This helps you to anticipate the language that will be used in French and makes it easier to understand what you hear.

Contrôle 2

I   You've heard about a local **propriété** (house where you can buy wine). You ask for directions. Listen and fill the gaps in English:

Take the .... direction; just after Saint-Pey-d'Armens take the .... on the .... After 5 km, turn .... At the village of Saint-Sulpice turn .... Carry on for .... metres. The house is on the right .... the river.

2   Listen to Camille Degrave being interviewed for her local radio station and tick the correct details below.

a   She lives in town   ■
              in the countryside   ■
              in a small village   ■
b   She lives next to the post office   ■
              next to the station   ■
              opposite the church   ■
c   She works in a shop   ■
              in an office   ■
              in a bank   ■
d   She is a dentist   ■
              a secretary   ■
              an architect   ■
e   She is 35   ■
              45   ■
              55   ■

3   Camille's company regularly receives visitors from its head office. Listen as her colleague tells Camille when to expect them and note down the dates.

M. Rolland, du .... **au** ....

M. Boulanger, du .... **au** ....

Mme Aubert, du .... **au** ....

Mlle Michaud, du .... **au** ....

4 Nicolas is now staying in a little village in Provence. How far away are the following towns? Listen and circle the right distance.

a	**Avignon**	**60 km, 62 km, 72 km**
b	**Marseille**	**45 km, 85 km, 95 km**
c	**Cannes**	**43 km, 83 km, 93 km**
d	**St-Tropez**	**78 km, 88 km, 98 km**

5 Listen to four people booking hotel rooms, and note the details in the boxes.

	no. of people	🚻	🛁
a			
b			
c			
d			

6 Read these questions and answers and choose a word from the box to fill the gap in each sentence.

parles
habite
travaille
travaillez
parle
habitez

a **Vous** .... **dans un magasin?**
   Non, je .... **chez moi.**
b **Tu** .... **anglais? Oui, et je** ....
   aussi allemand et français.
c **Vous** .... **ici? Oui, j'** .... **en ville.**

7 Which sign would you follow if . . .

a your car has broken down?
b you want a list of campsites in the area?
c you want a room for the night?
d you want to go swimming?
e you want to attend a religious service?
f you want to send a parcel?
g you want to catch a train?

Office du tourisme

HÔTEL

Garage

POSTE

PISCIN

gare SNCF

Église

8 You want to book a room in the Hôtel Royal in the summer.
Complete this fax to the manager, filling the gaps with the information
below.

a	April	*b*	a twin-bedded room
c	with bathroom	*d*	for four nights
e	28th June	*f*	2nd July
g	your name		

Cambridge, le 24 (a) ....

Monsieur,

Je voudrais réserver (b) ....

....

(c) ....,

(d) ....

du (e) ....

au (f) ....

au nom de (g) ....
Est-ce que vous pouvez confirmer la
réservation, s'il vous plaît?

Meilleures salutations,

(g) ....

9 Can you complete the following grid?

Across
2 Vous habitez en ville ou à la ....?
5 C'est ....? Non, c'est à 200 mètres.
9 C'est pour six jours ou une ....?
11 Il y a un parking à .... de l'église.
12 Je suis secrétaire. Mon .... est en ville.
13 Vous .... anglais? (speak)
15 Ma chambre est au premier ....
16 Il y a .... magasins près d'ici?

Down
1 Ma voiture est dans le ....
3 Prenez la première à droite, ... la deuxième à gauche.
4 Je .... travaille pas.
6 Octobre, ..., décembre.
7 Il habite dans un petit ....
8 Je suis infirmière à l' ....
10 Il y .... a deux.
14 Je voudrais une chambre pour .... 3 juin.

8

HUIT

À quelle heure vous ouvrez?

- **understanding opening hours**
  - **. . . and making enquiries**
- **enquiring about timetables**
- **checking travel details**

En France . . .

most shops close for lunch and then open again until around 7 p.m. On Sundays and Mondays, most small shops are closed except for **les boulangeries** (bakers') and **les fleuristes** (florists').

You can be certain of catching a train to most places every day of the week, but if you want to get there fast your best option is to go on a TGV, **train à grande vitesse** (high-speed train), at speeds of up to 300 km per hour. Whatever train you take, don't ignore the sign **COMPOSTEZ VOTRE BILLET** in the station, reminding you to punch your ticket in an orange-red pillar; otherwise your ticket is not valid.

Understanding opening hours . . .

1 Listen to these key phrases.

À quelle heure vous ouvrez?	What time do you open?
On ouvre à 7 heures	We open at 7 o'clock
. . . à 8 heures	. . . at 8 o'clock
À quelle heure vous fermez?	What time do you close?
On ferme à midi	We close at 12 noon

En français . . .

on (one) is very often used to mean 'we'. The verb which follows has the same ending as **il/elle**:

ici on parle anglais   we speak English here/English spoken here

2 Mélanie asks what time the baker's and the post office open tomorrow. Listen to the conversations and tick the right answers.

La boulangerie	**6.00**	**8.00**	**9.00**
La poste	**7.00**	**8.00**	**9.00**

En français . . .

when talking about the time of day, the key word is **heure(s)**.

à trois/3 heures	at 3 o'clock
à dix-neuf/19 heures	at 7 p.m./19.00 hours

Minutes are simply added to these . . .

à neuf heures quarante-cinq	at 9.45
à dix-neuf heures vingt	at 7.20 p.m./19.20

3 Listen to three shop assistants saying when the shop opens and match each assistant's answer with the right time, e.g. *1a*

09:30	08:30	14:15
a	*b*	*c*

. . . and making enquiries

4   Listen to these key phrases.

C'est fermé aujourd'hui	It's closed today
C'est ouvert le dimanche?	Is it open on Sundays?
Quand . . . ?	When . . . ?
Le château est ouvert . . .	The castle is open . . .
. . . tous les jours	. . . every day
. . . sauf le lundi	. . . except on Mondays

lundi Monday	**jeudi** Thursday
mardi Tuesday	**vendredi** Friday
mercredi Wednesday	**samedi** Saturday
	dimanche Sunday

5   Mélanie now asks at the local grocer's whether they're open on Sundays. Listen and tick the right box. **Après-midi** means 'afternoon' and **matin** means 'morning'.

Dimanche matin:	ouvert ■	fermé ■
Dimanche après-midi:	ouvert ■	fermé ■

6   She then enquires about opening hours for the castle and the museum. Listen and complete the details below.

	opening hours	day(s) closed
Château	....	....
Musée	....	....

Enquiring about timetables

1   Listen to these key phrases.

À quelle heure . . .	At what time . . .
. . . part le prochain train?	. . . does the next train leave?
. . . part le prochain car?	. . . does the next coach leave?
À quelle heure est-ce qu'il arrive?	At what time does it arrive?
Quand est-ce qu'il arrive?	When does it arrive?

2   Mélanie wants to visit Perpignan. Listen to her enquiring about train times and complete the details missing from the table below.

	1	2	3
Départ *(Departure)*	14.25	....	15.45
Arrivée *(Arrival)*	....	15.25	....

3   Now listen as she enquires about trains to the next village, Port-Vendres, famous for its fish market. Tick the right answer.

    a   What is the best way for her to get there? (**En** means 'by'.)

en car ■   **en train** ■   **en bus** ■

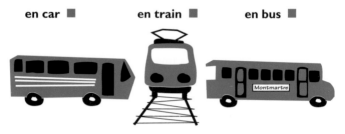

    b   Where does the next coach leave from?

place du Marché	■
place Saint-Jean	■
rue du Marché	■

    c   What time does the next coach leave?

12.00 ■   **12.15** ■   **12.30** ■

Checking travel details

1 Listen to these key phrases.

un billet pour Paris	a ticket to Paris
un aller simple	a single
un aller retour	a return
en première (classe)	first (class)
en seconde (classe)	second (class)
C'est quel quai?	Which platform is it?
Il faut changer à . . .	You have to change at . . .

2 Listen to four snatches of conversation at the ticket office. Tick the correct details you hear.

a single ■ return ■

b first class ■ second class ■

c platform 3 ■ platform 7 ■ platform 10 ■

d change at Nice ■ Marseille ■

En français . . .

il faut means 'it's necessary to', 'you have to' or 'we have to'.
Il faut réserver? Is it necessary to book?
Il faut aller à Nice. You have to go to Nice.

3 Can you ask for the following tickets?

a A single to Paris, second class

b Two returns to Nice, second class

c A single to Calais, first class

Put it all together

1   Match up the two halves of these sentences.

     a   **Je voudrais un aller**   le prochain train?
     b   **Un aller retour**   pour Nice, s'il vous plaît.
     c   **À quelle heure part**   à midi quinze.
     d   **Le train part**   à Lyon.
     e   **Il faut changer**   simple pour Paris.

2   Fill the gaps with the words from the list.

     a   **Il faut .... à Marseille.**
     b   **Il .... réserver?**
     c   **Un aller ...., s'il vous plaît.**
     d   **À quelle heure vous .... le dimanche?**

> faut
> ouvrez
> changer
> retour

3   Read these signs: what do they mean?

     a
> **FERMÉ**
> **LE MERCREDI**

     b
> **OUVERT**
> **TOUS LES JOURS**
> **SAUF LE JEUDI**

     c
> **ICI ON PARLE**
> **ANGLAIS**

4   Using **Il faut .... ?** how would you ask:

     a   if you have to book?
     b   if it's necessary to change in Paris?
     c   if you have to go to Port-Vendres?

Now you're talking!

I Imagine you're in a French railway station enquiring about timetables.

◆ Greet the lady at the desk and ask what time the next train for Boulogne leaves.
◇ **À 15 h 15.**
◆ Ask what time it arrives.
◇ **À 18 h 50.**
◆ Ask her to speak more slowly.
◇ **Oui. À 18 h 50.**
◆ Ask if you have to change.
◇ **Oui. Il faut changer à Paris.**
◆ Say you would like a single ticket, second class.
◇ **Voilà, monsieur.**
◆ Ask how much it is.
◇ **Ça fait 32,90 €.**
◆ Ask for the platform.
◇ **Quai six.**

2 You're at the baker's and enquire about opening hours.

◆ Greet the baker (a man).
◇ **Ah, bonjour.**
◆ Ask what time they open.
◇ **À 6 h 30.**
◆ Ask what time they close.
◇ **On ferme de 13 h à 15 h.**
◆ Ask whether it's open on Sundays.
◇ **Dimanche matin, oui, mais pas dimanche après-midi.**
◆ Say you don't understand and ask him to repeat.
◇ **Dimanche matin c'est ouvert, mais dimanche après-midi, c'est fermé.**

Quiz

1   Does the sign FERMÉ LE DIMANCHE mean 'closed on Sundays' or 'closed on Mondays'?

2   If it was **midi**, what time would it be?

3   What might happen if you ignore the sign COMPOSTEZ VOTRE BILLET?

4   Is **un car** a coach, a car or a train?

5   How do you say '8 a.m.' in French?

6   What day comes after **mercredi**?

7   If you travel on the train **tous les jours**, do you travel every week or every day?

8   If you are told **Il faut payer un supplément**, what do you think you have to do?

Now check whether you can . . .

- ask about opening times and days

- ask when the next train, bus or coach leaves and arrives . . .

   . . . and understand the answer – using the 24-hour clock

- understand what day of the week something is available

- ask for a train ticket

- check essential travel details

You now know that a number of French and English words, such as **train**, **classe**, **changer**, are very much alike. But, as you have seen in this unit, you also have to look out for **faux amis** (false friends) which mislead you into thinking you know what they mean – **car** (coach), **quai** (platform), **composter** (to punch). Look out too for **location**, which means 'hire'.

Je voudrais du fromage, s'il vous plaît

- **buying food and drink**

  . . . and asking for more (or less)
- **saying how much you need**
- **buying stamps and newspapers**

En France . . .

there are over 340 different cheeses. If you'd like to try lesser-known ones, look out for a **crémerie** (specialist cheese shop) or for the cheese stall at the market.

Ready-made dishes and salads to take away can be bought in a **charcuterie**, originally a specialist shop for ham, salami and other pork products.

You can buy stamps in most shops selling postcards. Newsagents don't always sell cigarettes; you buy these at a **bureau de tabac**. Supermarkets don't sell medicines. If you run out of aspirin, go to **la pharmacie** (the chemist's), recognisable by a green cross.

Buying food and drink . . .

I   Listen to these key phrases.

Je voudrais . . .	I'd like . . .
. . . du pain	. . . (some) bread
. . . du fromage	. . . (some) cheese
. . . de la viande	. . . (some) meat
. . . des œufs	. . . (some) eggs

2   Caroline is in the **alimentation** (general food shop). Listen as she goes through her shopping list, and tick off the items as you hear them mentioned. Can you add the item she buys that's missing from the list?

> **du pain**   bread
> **du beurre**   butter
> **de la confiture**   jam
> **du thé**   tea
> **du jambon**   ham
> **des œufs**   eggs
> **de la viande**   meat

En français . . .

du, de la, de l' and **des** all mean 'some':

du pain	some bread
de la viande	some meat
de l'eau	some water
des œufs	some eggs

Although the word 'some' is often left out in English e.g. 'cheese and wine', it is always included in French – **du fromage et du vin**

3   Caroline is now at the **boulangerie**, buying some croissants. Does she choose normal ones – **croissants nature** – or some with extra butter – **croissants au beurre**?

4   How would you say you'd like some of the following:

- bread?
- jam?
- eggs?

. . . and asking for more (or less)

5 Listen to these key phrases.

Et avec ceci/ça?	Anything else?
Comme ça?	Like this?
Un peu plus	A little bit more
Un peu moins	A little bit less
Ce sera tout	That will be all

6 Caroline is in the **crémerie** buying two kinds of cheese – **roquefort** and **gruyère**. Listen and link each of the assistant's questions (on the left) with Caroline's replies (on the right).

a	**Madame, vous désirez?**	**Du roquefort, s'il vous plaît.**
b	**Comme ça?**	**Un peu moins.**
c	**Voilà. Et avec ceci?**	**Ce sera tout, merci.**
d	**Comme ça?**	**Je voudrais du gruyère, s'il vous plaît.**
e	**Bien. Et avec ça?**	**Un peu plus, s'il vous plaît.**

7 Listen to Paul buying some **brie**. In reply to **Comme ça?**, does he ask for more or less? And what else does he buy?

8 How many French cheeses can you name in French? Look out for them in your local supermarket. Make a list and practise asking for them. You use **du** for all cheeses except those that start with a vowel e.g. **de l'emmenthal**.

Saying how much you need

1   Listen to these key phrases.

Cent grammes	100 grams
Deux cent cinquante grammes de fraises	250 grams of strawberries
Une demi-livre de tomates	Half a pound of tomatoes
Une livre de champignons	A pound of mushrooms
Un kilo de pommes de terre	A kilo of potatoes

2   Caroline is at the **magasin de fruits et légumes** (greengrocer's). Number the items below in the order you hear her ask for them.

bananes   *pommes*   *pêches*   *fraises*   *champignons*   *tomates*   *pommes de terre*

3   She then goes to the **alimentation** for the following items. Listen to find which quantity goes with which item. You'll need to know **une tranche de** (a slice of) and **une boîte de** (a tin of).

a	**une boîte de . . .**	pâté
b	**250 g de . . .**	jambon
c	**une tranche de . . .**	pêches
d	**quatre tranches de . . .**	gruyère
e	**un kilo de . . .**	sardines

Buying stamps and newspapers

1   Listen to these key phrases.

Vous vendez . . .	Do you sell . . .
. . . des journaux anglais?	. . . English newspapers?
. . . des cartes postales?	. . . postcards?
. . . des timbres pour l'Angleterre?	. . . stamps for England?
C'est joli	It's nice/pretty
C'est trop cher	It's too expensive
Je prends . . .	I'll have . . .

2   Paul is at the **marchand de journaux** (newsagent's). He has seen some German newspapers and wants to know whether they have English ones as well. They'll have some tomorrow, but when exactly?

3   Now listen as he asks about a pen he has seen.

    a   How much does it cost?
    b   Can he afford it?

4   Paul has chosen some rather expensive postcards. Listen as he buys some of them and some stamps.

How many postcards does he buy?	*a* 5	*b* 4	*c* 2
How much money does he spend?	*a* 2,12 €	*b* 2,82 €	*c* 2,92 €

En français . . .

you use **à** when you want to say what price something is

un timbre à 46 centimes   a 46-centime stamp

Put it all together

1 Béatrice is buying some salami. Read the dialogue and fill the gaps.
Celui-là means 'that one.'

Béatrice	**Bonjour, madame. Je .... du saucisson.**
Mme Chaillou	**Oui.**
Béatrice	**Quatre .... de celui-là.**
Mme Chaillou	**Quatre tranches de saucisson. Oui. Avec ...., madame?**
Béatrice	**Ce sera ...., merci.**

2 You need to buy a few things for a picnic. How would you ask for:

a	some bread?	*b*	250 grams of brie?
c	a tin of pâté?	*d*	some butter?
e	three slices of ham?	*f*	a kilo of tomatoes?
g	a kilo of bananas?	*h*	two bottles of mineral water?

3 Can you link these French shop signs to their English equivalents?

a **BOULANGERIE**
b **MARCHAND DE JOURNAUX**
c **ALIMENTATION**
d **FRUITS ET LÉGUMES**
e **CRÉMERIE**

newsagent's
general food shop
cheese shop
greengrocer's
baker's

4 Unscramble the letters on the right to find items for sale in these shops.

a	**Crémerie**	MAGROFE
b	**Épicerie**	NABJOM
c	**Boulangerie**	OSCRINTAS
d	**Fruits et légumes**	MOMSEP

Now you're talking!

1 Imagine you're at the grocer's.

- ◇ **Vous désirez?**
- ◆ Ask for a kilo of potatoes.
- ◇ **Oui. Avec ceci?**
- ◆ Half a pound of apples.
- ◇ **Voilà.**
- ◆ Ask if they sell ham.
- ◇ **Oui.**
- ◆ Say you'd like four slices.
- ◇ **Très bien. Et avec ça?**
- ◆ Ask for some brie.
- ◇ **Oui. Comme ça?**
- ◆ Ask for a bit less.
- ◇ **Voilà.**
- ◆ Ask for six eggs and a tin of pâté.
- ◇ **Bien.**
- ◆ Say that's all and ask for the price.
- ◇ **Ça fait 8,50 €.**
- ◆ Give the money – say 'there you are'.

2 You're out buying postcards when you see a leather wallet.

- ◆ Say it's nice and ask how much it is.
- ◇ **36 €.**
- ◆ Say it's too expensive and that you'll have the postcards.
- ◇ **Alors, deux cartes postales.**
- ◆ Ask whether they sell stamps.
- ◇ **Oui. Alors deux cartes postales et deux timbres à 46 centimes.**
- ◆ Ask how much that is.
- ◇ **Ça fait 1,22 €.**

Quiz

1 What can you buy in a **charcuterie**?
2 Would you buy a **camembert** in a **crémerie**?
3 If you're a vegetarian, which of the following can you eat:
   des pommes de terre, **du jambon**, **de la viande**?
4 How many **grammes** are there in **un kilo**?
5 What is a **saucisson**?
6 If something is **trop cher**, can you afford it?
7 Is **un peu moins** a bit more or a bit less?
8 If you want **des timbres**, would you go to a **pharmacie**?

Now check whether you can . . .

■ ask for common food items

■ say how much you require

■ ask for more or less

■ buy stamps and newspapers

■ recognise common shop signs

When learning a language, it can be very easy to underestimate how much you know. Go back occasionally to one of the very early units to prove to yourself how much French you've learnt. Think also about what you find easy . . . and difficult. If you can identify your strengths and weaknesses, you can build on the strengths and find ways of compensating for the weaknesses.

Bon appétit!

- enquiring about snacks
- reading a menu
- ordering a meal
- saying what you like and don't like

En France . . .

most cafés offer snacks: sandwiches, **croque-monsieur** (toasted cheese and ham sandwich) and **omelettes**. Cafés tend to stay open all day but many restaurants have very short opening hours, especially at lunch time. The most reliable time to have a hot meal is between 12 and 1.30 p.m. and between 7.30 and 9.30 p.m.

If you are a vegetarian, do not expect to see **des plats végétariens** (vegetarian dishes) on the menu. But most cooks will be happy to serve **une assiette de crudités** (a selection of raw vegetables.)

Enquiring about snacks

1 Listen to these key phrases.

Qu'est-ce que c'est?	What is it?
C'est un croque-monsieur avec un œuf	It's a toasted cheese and ham sandwich with an egg
Qu'est-ce que vous avez comme sandwichs?	What do you have in the way of sandwiches?
Qu'est-ce que vous avez comme glaces?	What do you have in the way of ice creams?

2 Barbara is in a café and wants to know what a **croque-madame** is. Listen and tick the right answer.

Qu'est-ce que c'est, un croque-madame?

a a toasted cheese sandwich
b a toasted cheese and ham sandwich
c a toasted cheese and ham sandwich with an egg

3 Paul and his sons are in a **salon de thé** (teashop). They order something to eat. Listen and tick any of these items that they order.

✓*a* **un sandwich au saucisson**   *b* **un sandwich au fromage**
✓*c* **une glace à la vanille**   *d* **une glace à la fraise**
✓*e* **une glace au chocolat**   ✓*f* **un sandwich au jambon**
g **une glace au citron**

En français . . .

the main ingredient or flavour is usually preceded by:
au for a masculine noun:
  une glace au chocolat   chocolate ice cream
à la for a feminine noun:
  une glace à la vanille   vanilla ice cream
à l' before a vowel or **h**:
  un gâteau à l'orange   orange cake

Reading a menu

1 Listen to these key phrases.

Vous avez choisi?   **Have you chosen?**
Vous prenez . . . ?   **Will you have . . . ?**
Je prends . . .   **I'll have . . .**
Le menu à 15 €   **The set menu at 15 euros**
Comme entrées . . .   **For starters . . .**

2 Fabien Degrave is taking his wife and a friend out to celebrate her birthday. Does she want a set menu or to eat **à la carte**?

En français. . .

verbs like **prendre** (to take/to have) which end in **-re** follow a slightly different pattern from those ending in **-er** (page 46). Look out in this unit for **je prends, tu prends** and **vous prenez.**

3 Read the set menu they're given, then listen and tick the starters they order.

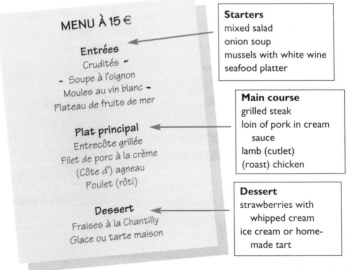

MENU À 15 €

Entrées
Crudités
Soupe à l'oignon
Moules au vin blanc
Plateau de fruits de mer

Plat principal
Entrecôte grillée
Filet de porc à la crème
(Côte d') agneau
Poulet (rôti)

Dessert
Fraises à la Chantilly
Glace ou tarte maison

Starters
mixed salad
onion soup
mussels with white wine
seafood platter

Main course
grilled steak
loin of pork in cream
    sauce
lamb (cutlet)
(roast) chicken

Dessert
strawberries with
    whipped cream
ice cream or home-
    made tart

Ordering a meal

1 Listen to these key phrases.

Comme plat principal? For your main course?
Et comme légumes? And for vegetables?
Et comme boisson? And to drink?
Tout de suite Right away
Bon appétit! Enjoy your meal!

2 At the Restaurant Gourmet, the waitress asks the Degrave party how they like their meat done. Listen and tick the boxes.

	saignant (rare)	à point (medium)	bien cuit (well done)
Fabien	✓		
Philippe			✓

3 She then asks for their vegetable order. Listen and tick their choices.

	haricots verts (beans)	petits pois (peas)	frites (chips)	salade (salad)
Thérèse	■	■	■	■
Fabien	■	■	■	■
Philippe	■	■	■	■

4 What drinks do they order? Tick the right answer.

a **bourgogne** ■ **bordeaux** ■ **côtes-du-rhône** ■
b **eau gazeuse** (sparkling water) ■
c **eau non-gazeuse** (still water) ■
d **une carafe d'eau** (jug of water) ■

5 Once the meal is over it's time to pay the bill – **l'addition**. Listen and find out whether they want any coffees first.

Saying what you like and don't like

1 Listen to these key phrases.

J'aime . . .	I like . . .
Je n'aime pas . . .	I don't like . . .
C'est délicieux!	It's delicious!
C'est très bon!	It's very good!
Ce n'est pas bon!	It's not very nice!
La cuisine est excellente!	The cooking is excellent!

2 Michel and Sabine are talking about the 15-euro menu. What do they like most? **Hors-d'œuvre** is another word for 'starters'.

	Hors-d'œuvre	Plat principal
Sabine	....	....
Michel	....	....

En français. . .

unlike in English, you use **le, la, les** when saying what you like and dislike:

J'aime la viande rouge	I like red meat
Je n'aime pas les fruits de mer	I don't like seafood

3 Now listen to three people describing what they like and don't like. Link each adjective on the left to the item on the right.

a **délicieux** — **le bœuf bourguignon** (beef in red wine)
b **très bon** — **le poulet rôti**
c **excellent** — **le service**
d **parfait** (perfect) — **le sorbet au cassis** (blackcurrant sorbet)
e **excellente** — **le gâteau au chocolat**
f **pas bon** — **la cuisine**

4 Now say in French what food and drink you like and don't like.

Put it all together

1 Match up the two halves of the sentences.

a	**Le poulet rôti**	**bien cuit, s'il vous plaît.**
b	**Je prends un steak**	**café, fraise ou cassis?**
c	**Qu'est-ce que vous avez**	**des haricots verts.**
d	**Qu'est-ce que c'est,**	**les fraises.**
e	**Je n'aime pas**	**le bœuf bourguignon?**
f	**Vanille, banane, chocolat,**	**est excellent!**
g	**Comme légumes, je prends**	**comme sandwichs?**

2 Martine is enquiring about dessert.
Fill the gaps using the words in the list on the right.

Martine	**Qu'est-ce que vous .... comme glaces?**
Serveur	**Vanille, ..., chocolat ou café.**
Martine	**Et .... tartes?**
Serveur	**De la .... aux pommes.**
Martine	**Je .... de la tarte aux pommes.**

prends
fraise
avez
comme
tarte

3 If you were in Paris, what would you say to find out a café's selection of the following?

a sandwiches   b omelettes   c ice cream

4 Put the following under the right heading:

petits pois   fraises   moules   glace   poulet   haricots verts
bœuf   soupe   pommes   agneau   champignons   crudités

Entrées	Viandes	Légumes	Desserts
....	....	....	....
....	....	....	....
....	....	....	....

Now you're talking!

1 Imagine you're in a restaurant in Cannes with a French friend. You've already seen the menu when the waiter greets you.

◇ **Bonjour, vous avez choisi?**
◆ Say you'd like two 15 € menus.
◇ **Bien. Qu'est-ce que vous prenez comme entrées?**
◆ Ask for one pâté and one soup.
◇ **Et comme plat principal?**
◆ Ask what a 'poulet basquaise' is.
◇ **C'est du poulet cuit dans une sauce tomate avec des poivrons** (peppers).
◆ Order one chicken and one steak.
◇ **Steak saignant, à point ou bien cuit?**
◆ Ask for 'medium'.
◇ **Bien. Et comme légumes?**
◆ Order some chips.
◇ **Et comme boisson?**
◆ Order a bottle of white wine and a bottle of sparkling mineral water.
◇ **Parfait.**

2 The starters have arrived.

◆ Tell your friend to enjoy his meal.
◇ **Merci. Toi aussi.**
◆ During the meal, you mention that the chicken is delicious.
◇ **Mon steak est excellent!**
◆ A little later, the waiter asks about dessert.
◇ **Vous désirez du fromage ou un dessert?**
◆ Ask what they have in the way of ice cream.
◇ **Vanille, fraise, ou café.**
◆ Order one coffee ice cream and one cheese.

Sometime later you call the waiter; ask for two coffees and the bill.

Quiz

1 Is an **hors-d'œuvre** a starter or a dessert?
2 What's the best time to have lunch in a French restaurant?
3 If the waiter says **Bon appétit!** does he want your order?
4 What is **l'addition**?
5 Is a **tarte aux fraises** an apple tart?
6 What's the difference between a **croque-monsieur** and a **croque-madame**?
7 What choice do you have if you see **Fromage ou dessert** on the menu?
8 Your meal is delicious. What would you say?

Now check whether you can . . .

■ order snacks and ice creams

■ read a simple menu

■ say what you want for starters, main course and dessert

■ say how you want your meat cooked

■ ask for the bill

■ say what you like and don't like

■ comment on the quality of the food

Bravo! Well done. You have completed *Talk French*.
And now prepare yourself for **Contrôle 3**, the final checkpoint which covers elements from the whole course, with some revision. Listen again to the conversations on the audio, test your knowledge of key phrases by covering up the English and use the quizzes and checklists on the final pages of each unit to assess how much you remember.

Contrôle 3

Imagine you have just arrived in France on holiday . . .

1 After a long drive, you stop at a café. You're feeling tired and you want to find out if there's a hotel nearby. Which of the following questions do you ask the waiter?

   a **Où est l'hôtel de ville?**
   b **Il y a un hôtel près d'ici?**
   c **Où est l'hôtel?**

2 You also want to ask the waiter whether you can use the telephone. What do you say?

   a **Vous voulez téléphoner?**
   b **Il faut téléphoner?**
   c **Je peux téléphoner?**

3 The waiter explains where the hotel is. Listen and make a note of the directions he gives you.

C'est loin?

....
....

How far away is it? ....

4 You finally arrive at your hotel and go to reception.

   a How would you say you'd like a double room?

     ....

   Listen to the receptionist's reply.

   b What type of room does she offer you?
   c What is the number of your room?
   d Which floor is it on?

5 At the hotel reception you pick up a restaurant card. Check any
words you don't know in the glossary.

Restaurant

LA TAVERNE

15 € MENUS 20 €

Spécialités régionales
Poissons et viandes grillés
Salle climatisée et belle terrasse
Concert de flamenco le jeudi soir
Ouvert tous les jours sauf le lundi

a What kind of food does this restaurant offer?
b Would you go there on a very hot day? Why?
c Which day would you go if you enjoy flamenco?
d Which day is their closing day?

6 You decide to give the restaurant a try. You overhear the people at
the next table ordering their meal. Listen and tick the correct options.

a The woman wants her steak . . .
   rare ■   medium ■   well done ■

b For vegetables, they choose . . .
   two portions of green beans ■
   one portion of green beans, one portion of chips ■
   one portion of chips ■

c To drink, they order . . .
   red wine and sparkling mineral water ■
   white wine and still mineral water ■
   red wine and a jug of water ■

7 You fancy a boat trip, **une promenade en mer**. You see
the following advertisement: read it through, then answer
the questions below.

> ## Les transports maritimes
> ## ALBATROS
> **Renseignements et Réservations**
> aux billetteries de Collioure de 10 h à 12 h et de 13 h 30 à 19 h.
>
> | | |
> |---|---|
> | **Promenade en mer:** | Toutes les heures (durée: 50 minutes) |
> | **Promenade de nuit:** | Avec musique et cocktail, tous les soirs, départ à 22 h. |

a How often do the boat trips leave?
b How long does the boat trip last?
c When does the night boat leave?
d When can you make a booking?

8 You decide to go on one of the boat trips and you shop for a picnic in
the local village shop. You also need some stamps for your postcards
home. How would you ask for the items pictured below?

9 Later in the week, you decide to visit Paris for the day, but you don't want to drive there. At the railway station how would you ask . . .

    a the time of the next train for Paris?
    b what time it arrives?
    c if it's necessary to change?
    d for a return ticket?

10 During the train journey you strike up a conversation with the man sitting next to you, who comes from Switzerland. What would you tell him and what questions would you ask, using **vous**, to obtain the following replies?

a ....
    Non, je suis suisse.

b ....
    J'habite à la campagne.

c ....
    Enchanté. Philippe Pasquier.

d ....
    Non, je ne parle pas anglais.

e ....
    Je suis architecte.

f ....
    Non. Je suis divorcé.

g ....
    Oui. J'ai une fille.

h ....
    Elle a 14 ans.

i ....
    Charlotte.

Now, he asks you some questions. Listen and be guided by the presenters on the audio.

Audio scripts and answers

This section contains transcripts of all the conversations. Answers which consist of words and phrases from the conversations are given in bold type in the transcripts. Other answers are given separately, after each activity.

Unit 1 Bonjour! Ça va?

Pages 8 & 9 Saying hello and goodbye

2 • Bonjour, **madame**.
  • Bonjour, **Mademoiselle Canal**.
  • Bonjour, monsieur.
  • Ah, bonjour, **Madame Martinot**.

3 • **Bonsoir**, Monsieur Faux.
  • Bonsoir, madame.
  • Bonsoir, mademoiselle.

4 • **Salut**, Marc! Ça va?
  • **Salut**, Julien! **Ça va.**

5 • Bonjour, madame.
  • Bonjour, monsieur.
  • Salut, Luc.

7 • Au revoir, **monsieur**.
  • **Au revoir**, madame. Et merci!
  • Au revoir, **madame**.
  • Au revoir, madame. **Merci!**

8 • Bonne nuit, **Pierre**!
  • Bonne nuit, Julien!
  • Bonne nuit, **Danièle**!
  • Bonne nuit, Julien! Merci!

9 • Bonjour, monsieur.
  • Ça va?
  • Merci, madame.
  • Au revoir, mademoiselle.

Pages 10 & 11 **Asking someone's name and introducing yourself**

2 • Comment vous appelez-vous? **(1)**
  • François Suret. **(2)** Et vous? **(3)**
    Je m'appelle Camille Dupuis. **(4)**
    Enchanté. **(5)**

3 • Comment tu t'appelles?
  • Julie. Et toi, comment **tu** t'appelles?
  • Je **m'appelle** Mélanie.

4 • Vous êtes Mademoiselle Marty?
  • Non.
  • Oh, Excusez-moi.
  • Vous êtes Mademoiselle Marty?
  • Non.
  • Excusez-moi.

6 • Mademoiselle Marty?
  • Oui, je **m'appelle** Arlette Marty.
  • Je **suis** Monsieur Bruno. Enchanté, **mademoiselle**.
  • **Enchantée,** Monsieur Bruno.

Using the numbers 0 to 10

2 1 10 3 5 6

Page 12 Put it all together

1 *a* Merci; *b* Comment vous appelez-vous?; *c* Vous êtes . . . ?; *d* Je suis. . . ; *e* Bonsoir!; *f* Enchanté(e); *g* Ça va?; *h* Salut!

2 *a* Bonjour; *b* Bonsoir; *c* Salut; *d* Bonne nuit.

4 neuf; dix; six.

Page 13 Now you're talking!

1 • Ah, bonjour, madame!
  • **Vous êtes Madame Tubert?**
  • Oui.

- **Bonjour, madame. Je suis . . . .**
- Enchantée.
- **Enchantée.**
2 - Bonjour, madame!
   - **Bonjour! Comment tu t'appelles?**
   - Virginie. Et vous?
   - **Je m'appelle . . .**

3 - Bonsoir, madame.
   - **Bonsoir, monsieur, je suis . . .**
   - Enchanté. Pierre Larrot.
   - **Enchantée.**

4 - **Au revoir, Madame Tubert, au revoir Virginie, et merci.**
   - Au revoir . . .

Page 14 Quiz

1 To say hello, good morning or good afternoon; *2* tu; *3* Enchanté(e);
4 a good friend; *5* at night when going to bed; *6* Excusez-moi!; *7* Je suis . . . /
Je m'appelle . . . ; *8* Comment tu t'appelles?

Unit 2 Vous êtes d'où?

Page 16 Giving your nationality

2 *a* Je suis français.
   b Je suis anglaise.
   c Je suis canadien.
   d Je suis américain.
   e Je suis anglais.
   f Je suis australienne.

3 Allemagne – allemand(e); Angleterre – anglais(e); Canada – canadien(ne); Écosse – écossais(e); Espagne – espagnol(e); États Unis – américain(e); France – français(e); Irlande – irlandais(e); Pays de Galle – gallois(e).

Page 17 Saying where you're from

2 - Je suis de **Stirling**, en **Écosse**.

- Je suis de **Madrid**, en **Espagne**.
- Je suis de **Manchester**, en **Angleterre**.
3 - Marie-Pierre, vous êtes de Bayeux?
   - Non, je suis de **Bordeaux**.
   - Et vous M. Michaud, vous êtes de Nantes?
   - Non, je suis de **Nîmes**.

Page 18 Saying what you do for a living

2 - Quelle est votre profession?
   - Je suis **architecte**.
   - Et vous?
   - Je suis **ingénieur**.
   - Et vous? Quelle est votre profession?
   - Je suis **secrétaire**.

3 - Paul, quelle est votre profession?
   - Je ne travaille pas. Je suis **retraité**.
   - Et vous, quelle est votre profession?
   - Je suis **étudiant**.
   - Et vous, Marianne, vous êtes **étudiante**?
   - Excusez-moi, je ne **comprends** pas.

Page 19 Using the numbers 11 to 20

2 *a* quatorze; *b* douze; *c* dix-neuf;
   d seize; *e* quinze.

3 **12 19 13 20 14 11 15**
   Seize (16) *was not mentioned.*

4 *a* **14**; *b* **16**; *c* **11**; *d* **13**

Page 20 Put it all together

1 - Vous êtes française?
   - Non, non. Je suis anglaise.
   - Ah, vous êtes anglaise! Et vous êtes de Londres?
   - Non, je suis de Chichester.

2 *a* Je suis de Sydney, en Australie. Je suis australienne.
   b Je suis de Manchester, en Angleterre. Je suis anglaise.

c Je suis de Glasgow, en Écosse. Je suis écossais.
d Je suis de Nice, en France. Je suis français.
e Je suis de Los Angeles, aux États Unis. Je suis américaine.
f Je suis de Toronto, au Canada. Je suis canadienne.

3 France douze; Irlande quinze; pays de Galles onze; Angleterre quatorze; Canada dix-sept; États-Unis seize; Australie vingt; Allemagne dix-neuf.

4 a dix-neuf (19) b vingt (20)
c treize (13) d quatorze (14)

Page 21 Now you're talking!

1 ● Excusez-moi, monsieur, la gare s'il vous plaît.
● **Je ne suis pas de Toulouse.**
● Vous n'êtes pas français?
● **Non, je suis anglais.**
● Vous êtes d'où?
● **Je suis de Birmingham. Vous êtes d'où?**
● Je suis de Séville.
● **Je ne comprends pas.**
● Je suis de Séville. Je suis espagnole.

2 ● Bonjour, madame. Vous êtes américaine?
● **Non, je suis . . .**
● Vous êtes d'où?
● **Je suis de . . .**
● Comment vous appelez-vous?
● **Je m'appelle . . .**

3 ● Quelle est votre profession?
● **Je suis ingénieur. Quelle est votre profession?**
● Je suis professeur.

Page 22 Quiz

1 Je suis de Bristol; 2 a woman;
3 ne . . . pas 4 no; 5 fifteen; 6 the number of the department; 7 Je ne comprends pas;

8 américain

Unit 3 **Voici Émilie**

Pages 24 & 25 Introducing friends and family

2 ● Mon mari, Patrick.
● Ma femme, **Marion**, et mes amis, Émilie et Nicolas.
● Bonjour.

3 ● Voici **Benjamin**, mon mari. Il est **canadien**.
● Enchantée.
● Enchanté.

4 ● Vous êtes mariée?
● Je suis **divorcée**. Et vous?
● Je suis **célibataire**.

6 ● Isabelle, vous avez des enfants?
● Oui, j'ai **une fille**.
● Et vous, Émilie?
● **Non**, je n'ai pas d'enfants.
● Et vous, Marion, vous avez des enfants?
● Oui, j'ai trois enfants: **un fils** et **deux filles**.

7 ● Vous avez des enfants?
● Oui, j'ai une fille, Sabine, et un fils, Luc. Sabine a un fils, Jean-Claude. Luc n'a pas d'enfants.
She has one grandchild.

Page 26 Saying how old you are

2 21 vingt et un; 23 vingt-trois; 26 vingt-six; 30 trente; 38 trente-huit; 40 quarante; 45 quarante-cinq; 50 cinquante; 58 cinquante-huit; 60 soixante.

3 **25 33 40 42 58 67**

4 ● Tu as quel âge, Aurélien?
● J'ai **vingt et un** ans. (**21**)
● Et toi, Alex?
● J'ai **vingt** ans. (**20**)

- Et toi, Elisabeth?
- J'ai **seize** ans. (**16**)

5 • Madame Blanc, vous avez quel âge?
- **Quarante-cinq** ans. (45)
- Vous avez quel âge, Monsieur Blanc?
- J'ai **cinquante et un** ans. (51)

Page 27 **Talking about your family**

2 • Vous **avez** des enfants?
- Oui, j'ai une **fille**.
- Elle s'appelle comment?
- **Elle** s'appelle Valérie.
- Elle a quel **âge**?
- Elle **a** vingt et un **ans**.

3 • J'ai 55 ans. J'ai deux enfants: Gérard,
  mon fils, a 28 ans et Isabelle, ma fille,
  a 32 ans.
- Je suis mariée et j'ai une fille.
- Je suis divorcée. J'ai deux enfants:
  mon fils a 15 ans et ma fille a 16 ans.
  a Sabine *b* Alain *c* Catherine

Page 28 **Put it all together**

1 *a* Chantal; *b* mon frère; *c* 13 ans; *d* ma
  sœur; *e* Philippe; *f* ma femme.

2 *a* a; *b* avez; *c* ai; *d* as; *e* ai

3 *a* Je **m'appelle** Martine. *b* Mon **mari**
  s'appelle Marc. *c* J'ai un **fils** et une **fille**.
  Mon fils a **vingt-trois** ans. Il s'appelle
  Benoît. *e* Ma fille a **vingt et un ans**.
  Elle **s'appelle** Delphine.

Page 29 **Now you're talking!**

1 • Bonjour, madame. Comment vous
  appelez-vous?
- **Sophie Smith. Bonjour.**
- Vous êtes mariée?
- **Oui, voici mon mari, Michael.**
- Vous avez des enfants?
- **Oui, j'ai un fils et une fille.**
- Et votre fille, elle s'appelle comment?
- **Elle s'appelle Anna.**
- Elle a quel âge?

- **Elle a douze ans.**
- Et votre fils, il s'appelle comment?
- **Il s'appelle Martin.**
- Il a quel âge?
- **Il a quatorze ans.**

2 • **Vous êtes mariée?**
- Je suis divorcée.
- **Vous avez des enfants?**
- Oui, j'ai un fils, Théo.
- **Il a quel âge?**
- Il a quatorze ans. Ah, voici Théo!
- **Bonjour, Théo! Voici Martin et
  Anna.**

Page 30 **Quiz**

1 une fille; *2* mon; *3* célibataire;
4 Je n'ai pas d'enfants; *5* Elle a . . . ans;
6 Tu as quel âge?; *7* J'ai . . . ans; *8* 50.

Unit 4 **Un thé, s'il vous plaît**

Pages 32 & 33 **Ordering a drink in a café**

2 • Vous désirez, monsieur-dame?
- Un thé, s'il vous plaît.
- Oui. Nature, lait, citron?
- **Un thé au lait**, s'il vous plaît.
- Oui. Et pour monsieur?
- Pour moi, **un thé au citron**, s'il vous
  plaît.
- Très bien.

3 • Bonjour, messieurs-dames. Vous
  désirez?
- **Une bière**, s'il vous plaît.
- **Un café**, s'il vous plaît.
- Pour moi, **une eau minérale**, s'il
  vous plaît. Et **un jus d'orange** pour
  Christine.
- Alors, une eau minérale, un café, une
  bière, et un jus d'orange.

4 *a* Alors, un coca, une limonade et
  un thé au lait.
  b Un café, une pression et **un
  Schweppes**.
  c Alors, deux bouteilles de champagne.

d Un vin **rouge** et une eau minérale.

5 • Vous **désirez**?
   • Deux cafés, un **grand** café et un **café** crème.
   • Alors deux **cafés,** un **grand café** et un **café** crème.

Page 34 Offering, accepting or refusing a drink

2 • Vous **voulez** un apéritif, Madame Blois?
   • Non, merci. Pour moi, un verre d'eau.
   • Et vous, Monsieur Blois? Un apéritif?
   • Oui, **merci.**
   • Qu'est-ce que vous **désirez**? Un martini, un porto, un whisky?
   • Un porto, s'il vous plaît.
   • D'accord. **Voilà**. À votre santé!
   Porto is port.

Page 35 Asking the price of drinks

2   70 soixante-dix; 73 soixante-treize; 79 soixante-dix-neuf; 80 quatre-vingts; 81 quatre-vingt-un; 92 quatre-vingt-douze; 94 quatre-vingt-quatorze; 100 cent

3 • Une bouteille de vin, alors ça fait **treize euros, quatre-vingt-cinq (13,85 €)**. Un verre de champagne, **sept euros, soixante-dix (7,70 €)**. Deux martinis, ça fait **neuf euros, quatre-vingt (9,80 €)**.

4 *a* Monsieur, s'il vous plaît, c'est combien?
   Alors, un verre de champagne et un jus d'orange, ça fait **dix euros, quatre-vingts. (10,80 €)**
  b Monsieur, s'il vous plaît, c'est combien?
   Trois cocas, un Schweppes et un café crème, **douze euros, quatre-vingt-dix. (12,90 €)**
  c Monsieur, s'il vous plaît, c'est

combien?
Alors, deux bières, un verre de vin rouge et un café, ça fait **onze euros, soixante-quinze. (11,75 €)**

Page 36 Put it all together

1 *a* un café; *b* une bière; *c* un thé; *d* une limonade; *e* un coca; *f* un Orangina; *g* une eau minérale; *h* un jus de fruits.

2 *a* Qu'est-ce que vous désirez? Une limonade, s'il vous plaît.
  b C'est combien? Ça fait douze euros.
  c Vous désirez un thé au lait? Non, un thé au citron.
  d Vous voulez un jus de fruits? Oui, un jus d'orange.
  e Vous voulez un apéritif? Oui, un martini, s'il vous plaît.

3 • Vous désirez?
   • Un thé, s'il vous plaît.
   • Nature, lait, citron?
   • Au lait.
   • Voilà!
   • C'est combien?
   • Un euro, soixante.
   • Voilà. Merci.

4 *a* cinquante-deux (52); *b* quatre-vingts (80); *c* soixante-treize (73); *d* quatre-vingt-dix (90).

Page 37 Now you're talking!

1 • **Monsieur, s'il vous plaît!**
   • Bonjour, messieurs dames. Vous désirez?
   • **Un grand café, un thé et un jus d'orange.**
   • Très bien, merci.
   • **Merci, monsieur. C'est combien?**
   • Ça fait cinq euros, vingt.
   • **Voilà.**

2 • Madame, monsieur, bonjour. Vous désirez?
   • **Un coca et une bière.**

- Bouteille? Pression?
- **Pression, s'il vous plaît.**
- Très bien.
- **C'est combien?**
- Ça fait dix euros, soixante-dix.

3 • **Une bouteille de champagne, s'il vous plaît!**

4 • **Vous voulez un apéritif?**
- Oui, merci.
- **Qu'est-ce que vous désirez? Un martini ou un whisky?**
- Pour moi, un martini.
- Un whisky pour moi, s'il vous plaît.
- **Voilà. À votre santé!**

Page 38 **Quiz**

1 water – it's non-alcoholic; *2* un café crème; *3* café, coca, champagne; *4* 90; *5* pression; *6* À votre santé!; *7* The terrace, where you sit outside; *8* How much is it?; *9* Oui, merci.

Contrôle I (Pages 39–42)

1 *a* À votre santé! *b* Bonne nuit!
c Voilà! *d* Je ne comprends pas.
e Enchanté! *f* Excusez-moi. *g* Ça va?

2 *1* Votre nom, s'il vous plaît?
2 Madame Chevalier.
3 Et votre prénom?
4 **Christine.**
5 Votre adresse, s'il vous plaît?
6 **44** avenue de la Gare, 30100 Alès.
7 Et votre numéro de téléphone?
8 C'est le 04 **66** 98 35 **57.**

3 • Je m'appelle Rosanna. Je suis **espagnole** et je suis de **Barcelone.**
- Je m'appelle Wilfried. Je suis **allemand** et je suis de **Berlin.**
- Je m'appelle Elisabeth. Je suis **anglaise** et je suis de **Brighton.**
- Je m'appelle Nicole. Je suis **canadienne** et je suis de **Toronto.**

- Je m'appelle Paul. Je suis **anglais** et je suis de **Newcastle.**

4 • Vingt euros quarante-cinq.
- Sept euros, trente.
- Dix-sept euros, soixante-quinze.
- Quatorze euros, cinquante.
- Six euros, quatre-vingt-dix.
- Huit euros, soixante-quinze.
(so number the prices 4, 2, 6, 1, 3, 5)

5 Paris, Calais, Arles, Tarbes, Nîmes, Cahors.

6 • Bonjour. Vous désirez?
- **Un thé au lait, une bière et un verre d'eau, s'il vous plaît.**
- Très bien . . . La bière, pression ou bouteille?
- **Une bouteille, s'il vous plaît.**
- Vous êtes américaine?
- **Non, anglaise.**
- Vous êtes d'où?
- **Je suis de Bristol.**
- **C'est combien?**
- Ça fait 10,70 €.
- **Voilà. Merci.**

8 Dear Anna, My name is Julie. I am from Geneva, in Switzerland. I am 14. I have a brother and a sister. My sister is 18, she is an au pair in Germany. My brother is 23. He is in France. He is married but he doesn't have any children. My father is an architect and my mother is a French teacher.

9 Café crème, jus de fruits, coca, vin rouge, bière, thé.

Unit 5 **Où est la poste?**

Pages 44 & 45 **Asking where something is and how far it is**

2 • Où est le château, Virginie?
- C'est ici.
- Et le cinéma? Où est le cinéma?

- Le cinéma est en face de la gare.
- Où est le musée?
- Le musée est là.
- Et les magasins? Où sont les magasins, s'il vous plaît?
- Près de l'église.

4
- Pardon, mademoiselle. C'est loin, **la plage**?
- Non, c'est à **10 minutes**.
- Excusez-moi, madame. **Le marché . . .** c'est loin?
- Non. C'est à **100 mètres**.
- Pardon, monsieur. C'est loin, **le centre-ville**?
- C'est à **cinq minutes**, monsieur.

5 a ● Où est **la poste**, s'il vous plaît?
   ● À côté du café, monsieur.
   ● Merci, madame.
   b ● Pardon, madame. Où est **l'hôtel**?
   ● L'hôtel est avant la gare, monsieur.
   ● Merci beaucoup.
   c ● Pardon, madame. Où est le **café**?
   ● En face de l'église, monsieur.
   ● Merci.
   d ● Pardon, monsieur. Où est le **musée**?
   ● Le musée est après le château, monsieur.
   ● Merci, monsieur.
   e ● Pardon, mademoiselle. Où est l'église?
   ● C'est à trois **cents** mètres de la banque.

Pages 46 & 47 **Saying where you live and work**

2 ● Vous habitez où?
   ● J'habite **dans un petit village**.
   ● Et vous, madame. Vous habitez où?
   ● Moi aussi, j'habite **à la campagne**.
   ● Vous habitez où, monsieur?
   ● J'habite **en ville**.
   ● Moi, aussi.

3 ● Bernard, tu habites où?

- J'habite **en ville**.

5 ● Mon frère travaille **chez Peugeot**.
   ● Ma sœur travaille pour **une compagnie américaine**. Elle travaille **à Paris**.
   ● Et ma femme travaille **dans un bureau**.
   ● Moi, je travaille chez moi.

6 a ● Je ne travaille pas. Je suis **au chômage**.
   b ● Je suis **étudiant**.
   c ● Je suis **mère de famille**.
   d ● Je ne travaille pas. Je suis **retraité**.

Page 48 **Put it all together**

1 a gare; b musée; c château; d marché.

2 Lille est à soixante-dix-sept kilomètres. Boulogne est à quatre-vingts kilomètres. Le Touquet est à quatre-vingt-quinze kilomètres. Montreuil est à quatre-vingt-dix-huit kilomètres.

3 a le; b l'; c la; d le; e le; f la

Page 49 **Now you're talking!**

1 ● **Où est l'hôtel?**
   ● C'est là.
   ● **Où est le château?**
   ● Le château, c'est là, en face de la mairie.
   ● **C'est loin?**
   ● Non, c'est à cinq minutes d'ici.
   ● **Où sont le musée et l'église?**
   ● Alors, le musée est ici et l'église est là.

2 ● **Madame, s'il vous plaît. Un café au lait s'il vous plaît.**
   ● Bien, madame.
   ● **Où est la banque, s'il vous plaît?**
   ● C'est là, à cent mètres du café.
   ● **Vous habitez en ville?**
   ● Non, j'habite dans un petit village à la campagne.
   ● **C'est loin?**
   ● Non, c'est à 20 kilomètres.

3 • Vous êtes américaine?
  • **Je suis + *your nationality***
  • Vous êtes d'où?
  • **Je suis + *where you're from***
  • Vous habitez où?
  • **J'habite + *where you live***
  • Quelle est votre profession?
  • **Je suis + *your profession***
  • Vous travaillez où?
  • **Je travaille + *where you work***

Page 50 Quiz

1 the; *2* in an office; *3* après; *4* next to;
5 la gare; *6* quatre cents mètres; *7* C'est à
dix minutes; *8* magasin.

Unit 6 Il y a une piscine ici?

Pages 52 & 53 Asking for a specific place and making simple enquiries

2
a • Pardon, monsieur. Il y a des taxis ici?
    Oui, madame, **place de la République**.
b • Pardon, madame. Il y a un supermarché ici?
    • Oui, **place du Marché**.
c • Pardon, madame. Il y a une piscine ici?
    • Oui, il y a une piscine **rue de la Gare**.
    • Merci beaucoup, madame.
d • Excusez-moi, mademoiselle. Il y a des magasins ici?
    • Il y a des magasins **dans le centre-ville** à cinq cents mètres.
e • Pardon, madame. Il y a un camping ici?
    • Oui, **rue de Paris**, monsieur.
f • Pardon, mademoiselle. Il y a un parking ici?
    • Oui, **dans le centre-ville**.

3 • Pardon, mademoiselle. Il y a un camping ici?
  • Pardon, madame. Il y a une piscine ici?
  • Pardon, monsieur. Il y a une poste ici?
  • Pardon, monsieur. Il y a une banque ici?

5 • Excusez-moi, monsieur. **Ma voiture est en panne.** Est-ce qu'il y a un garage près d'ici?
  • À 12 km, madame.
  • Oh, c'est loin! Il y a **une cabine téléphonique** près d'ici?
  • Oui, il y en a une **là-bas**.

6
a • Pardon, madame. Est-ce qu'il y a une poste près d'ici?
    • Oui, monsieur. **En face de la banque.**
b • Pardon, madame. Est-ce qu'il y a un supermarché près d'ici?
    • Oui. **Là-bas, à côté de la banque**, madame.
c • Excusez-moi, monsieur. Il y a une cabine téléphonique ici?
    • Oui. **À côté de la poste**, madame.
    • Merci, monsieur.
d • Pardon, monsieur. Il y a un restaurant près d'ici?
    • Il y a une pizzeria **en face du supermarché**.
The map is not correct. The pizzeria is opposite the supermarket.

Pages 54 & 55 Understanding basic directions and asking for help to understand

2
a • Pardon, mademoiselle. Pour aller à l'Office du Tourisme?
    • Prenez **la première à droite** et c'est là, **à gauche**. (**B**)
b • Pardon, monsieur. Où est le marché, s'il vous plaît?
    • Allez **tout droit** et prenez **la deuxième à gauche**. (**F**)
c • Excusez-moi, monsieur. Où est l'hôpital, s'il vous plaît?

- Allez, allez **tout droit** et prenez **la troisième à droite. (D)**

3

a
- Pardon, monsieur. Où est la gare, s'il vous plaît?
- Allez **tout droit** et tournez **à droite après le pont.**

b
- Pardon, mademoiselle. Où est le cinéma, s'il vous plaît?
- Tournez **à gauche après le parking** et c'est **à gauche.**

c
- Excusez-moi, madame. Où est le camping, s'il vous plaît?
- Allez **tout droit** et tournez **à gauche après l'église et c'est à droite.**

5
- Pardon, madame. Pour aller à l'Hôtel de Bordeaux?
- **Continuez tout droit. Prenez la troisième à droite et c'est à 200 mètres à droite.**
- Oh. Vous pouvez parler plus lentement, s'il vous plaît?
- Continuez tout droit. Prenez la troisième à droite et c'est à 200 mètres à gauche.
- Merci beaucoup, madame.

- Pardon, monsieur. Le centre-ville, s'il vous plaît?
- **Tournez à droite et continuez tout droit. C'est à deux kilomètres.**
- Oh! . . . Vour pouvez répéter, s'il vous plaît?
- Alors, tournez à droite et continuez tout droit. C'est à deux kilomètres.

6
- Il y a une **piscine** ici?
- Oui, place de la République. Prenez la **deuxième** à droite, puis tournez **à gauche.**
- Vous pouvez **répéter**, s'il vous plaît?
- Oui, **prenez** la deuxième à droite, puis tournez à gauche. C'est **place** de la République.
- Merci, madame.

7
- Pardon, madame. Pour aller à la gare?
- Oui, alors **allez tout droit, prenez la troisième à gauche et c'est à deux cents mètres.**

8
- Pardon, il y a une banque près d'ici?
- Il y a un camping près de la gare?
- Vous pouvez répéter, s'il vous plaît?

Page 56 **Put it all together**

1 Pour; droit; tournez; deuxième; face; lentement.

2 The swimming pool is next to the campsite, opposite **E**.

4 *a* eau; *b* droite; *c* infirmière; *d* garage; *e* banque; *f* autoroute

Page 57 **Now you're talking!**

1
- **Pardon, madame, il y a un Office du Tourisme ici, s'il vous plaît?**
- Prenez la deuxième à droite et puis la première à gauche.
- **C'est loin?**
- Non, c'est à dix minutes.
- **Il y a une poste près d'ici?**
- Oui, il y en a une après la place du Marché, à gauche.
- **Vous pouvez répéter, s'il vous plaît?**
- La poste est après la place du Marché, à gauche.
- **Merci beaucoup et au revoir.**

2
- **Il y a une banque près d'ici?**
- Oui, il y en a trois. Il y en a une place du Marché.
- **Vous pouvez parler plus lentement, s'il vous plaît?**
- Il y a une banque place du Marché. Continuez tout droit et prenez la deuxième rue à gauche.
- **C'est loin?**
- Oh non, c'est à cinq minutes.
- **Il y a un cinéma ici?**

- Non, il n y'a pas de cinéma ici.
- **Merci, au revoir, monsieur.**

3 • Pardon. Il y a une banque près d'ici?
- **Il y a une banque là-bas, à droite.**
- Là-bas, à droite? C'est loin?
- **Non, c'est à deux minutes.**

Page 58 Quiz

1 il y a; *2* garage; *3* toll; *4* route départementale; *5* deuxième; *6* piscine; *7* en; *8* false: it means 'Could you speak more slowly?'

Unit 7 Je voudrais une chambre

Pages 60 & 61 Saying which type of room you want and how long you want it for

2 • Bonsoir, madame.
- Oui monsieur, qu'est-ce que vous désirez?
- Je voudrais une chambre pour une personne.
- Avec douche ou salle de bains?
- **Avec salle de bains**, s'il vous plaît.

3 • Bonsoir, monsieur.
- Bonsoir, madame. Je voudrais une chambre pour deux personnes.
- Oui. Une chambre avec deux lits ou avec un grand lit?
- **Un grand lit**, s'il vous plaît.
- Un grand lit.

4 *a* • J'ai une chambre avec douche au deuxième étage ou une chambre avec salle de bains au troisième étage.
- Je prends la chambre avec salle de bains au **troisième étage**, s'il vous plaît. (3e)
b • J'ai une chambre avec salle de bains au premier étage ou une chambre avec douche au quatrième étage.

- Je prends la chambre **au premier étage**. (1er)

5 • Je voudrais une chambre pour deux personnes avec douche.
- Je voudrais une chambre pour une personne avec douche et WC.
- Je voudrais une chambre avec deux lits, avec salle de bains et WC.

7 *a* Je voudrais une chambre pour deux personnes pour **trois nuits**, s'il vous plaît. (3 nights)
b Je voudrais une chambre pour une personne pour **demain** seulement. (tomorrow only)
c Je voudrais une chambre pour **ce soir**, s'il vous plaît. (tonight)
d Je voudrais une chambre pour **une semaine**. (1 week)

9 • Vous pouvez épeler votre nom, s'il vous plaît?
- BLANCHET.
His surname is **Blanchet.**

Pages 62 & 63 Booking a room and paying for it

2 *a* Je voudrais réserver une chambre pour **le trois (3) avril.**
b Je voudrais réserver une chambre **du premier au quatre (1–4) juin.**
c Je voudrais réserver une chambre pour **le quatorze (14) juillet.**
d Je voudrais réserver une chambre **du douze au quinze (12–15) août.**

3 Je voudrais une chambre . . . *a* pour le quinze juillet; *b* pour le dix avril; *c* pour le premier août; *d* du trois au six septembre; *e* du onze au quatorze mai; *f* du premier au quatre juin.

5/6
- Bonjour, monsieur.
- Bonjour, madame.
- Je voudrais une chambre, s'il vous plaît.

- C'est pour combien de personnes?
- Pour deux personnes, s'il vous plaît.
- Et pour combien de nuits?
- Pour trois nuits.
- Pour deux personnes, pour trois nuits . . . avec salle de bains?
- Oui. C'est combien?
- **Cent quinze euros**, madame. (**115 €**)
- Le petit déjeuner est compris?
- Ah non. Le petit déjeuner est en supplément, **huit euros** par personne. (**8 €**)
- Je peux payer avec une carte de crédit?
- Oui, madame.

7 • Je voudrais réserver une chambre pour deux personnes avec salle de bains pour une semaine.
  • C'est combien?
  • Le petit déjeuner est compris?
  • Je peux payer avec une carte de crédit?

Page 64 Put it all together

1 *a* Je voudrais une chambre pour deux personnes.
  b Je voudrais une chambre avec deux lits.
  c C'est pour une semaine.
  d Je peux payer avec une carte de crédit?
  e Le petit déjeuner est compris?
  f C'est 8 euros en supplément.
  g La chambre est au premier étage.
  h Vous pouvez épeler, s'il vous plaît?

2 *a* Je voudrais une chambre pour deux personnes pour une semaine.
  b Je voudrais une chambre pour une personne pour trois nuits.
  c Le petit déjeuner est compris?
  d Je voudrais une chambre au deuxième étage.

3 *a* yes – 6 €. *b* yes *c* no *d* no

Page 65 Now you're talking!

1 • **Bonjour, monsieur. Je voudrais une chambre pour ce soir.**
  • Oui, madame. Qu'est-ce que vous désirez?
  • **Je voudrais une chambre pour deux personnes.**
  • Très bien. Avec un grand lit ou avec deux lits?
  • **Avec deux lits.**
  • Bien. Avec salle de bains ou avec douche?
  • **Avec salle de bains. C'est combien?**
  • Une chambre pour deux personnes avec salle de bains, ça fait 60 euros.
  • **Le petit déjeuner est compris?**
  • Non, il est en supplément.
  • **C'est combien?**
  • Ça fait 6 euros 50 par personne.

2 • **Je voudrais réserver une chambre pour deux personnes avec deux lits et une douche pour le 22 juillet.**
  • Oui, madame.
  • **Je peux payer avec une carte de crédit?**
  • Oui, madame.
  • **C'est combien?**
  • Ça fait 53 euros, madame.

Page 66 Quiz

1 No, it's the town hall; *2* when they are full; *3* a douche; *4* au quatrième étage; *5* janvier, juin and juillet; *6* DEPUIS; *7* true; *8* une semaine.

Contrôle 2 (Pages 67–70)

1 Prenez la direction **Bordeaux**. Juste après St Pey d'Armens, prenez la **troisième à droite**. Après cinq kilomètres, tournez **à gauche**. Continuez tout droit. Au village Saint-

Sulpice, tournez **à droite**. Continuez pendant **500** mètres: la propriété est à droite **en face de** la rivière.

2 • Camille, vous habitez en ville ou à la campagne?
  • J'habite au centre d'**un petit village à la campagne**, juste **à côté de la poste**.
  • Et vous travaillez où?
  • Je travaille à Libourne, à 45 km.
  • Et vous travaillez dans une banque?
  • Non, je travaille **dans un bureau. Je suis secrétaire**.
  • Vous avez quel âge?
  • J'ai **trente-cinq ans**.

3 Alors, M. Rolland vient du **1ᵉʳ** au **5 mai**; M. Boulanger, du **27** au **30 juin**; Mme Aubert, du **13** au **15 juillet**; et Mlle Michaud, du **16** au **21 septembre**.

4 Avignon est à **72km**, Marseille est à **85km**, Cannes est à **93km** et St Tropez est à **78km**.

5
a • Bonsoir, monsieur. Je voudrais réserver **une chambre avec salle de bains pour deux personnes**, s'il vous plaît. (2 people with bath)
b • Bonsoir, madame. Je voudrais réserver **une chambre avec douche**. (1 person, with shower)
c • Bonjour, madame. Je voudrais réserver **deux chambres avec douche pour trois personnes** (3 people, 2 showers)
d • Bonjour, monsieur. Je voudrais réserver **une chambre pour une personne avec salle de bain**. (1 person, with bath)

6 a travaillez; travaille; b parles; parle c habitez; habite.

7 a GARAGE; b OFFICE DU TOURISME; c HÔTEL; d PISCINE; e ÉGLISE; f POSTE; g GARE SNCF.

8 a avril; b une chambre avec deux lits; c avec salle de bains; d pour quatre nuits; e 28 juin; f 2 juillet.

9 Across
  2 campagne; 5 loin; 9 semaine; 11 côté; 12 bureau; 13 parlez; 15 étage; 16 des
  Down
  1 garage; 3 puis; 4 ne; 6 novembre; 7 village; 8 hopitâl; 10 en; 14 le

Unit 8 À quelle heure vous ouvrez?

Pages 72 & 73 Understanding opening hours and making enquirie

2 • Pardon, madame. À quelle heure vous ouvrez demain?
  • On ouvre **à 6 heures**.
  • Pardon, monsieur. À quelle heure vous ouvrez?
  • On ouvre la poste **à 9 heures**, madame.

3 a On ouvre à **neuf heures trente**.
  b On ouvre à **quatorze heures quinze**.
  c On ouvre à **huit heures trente**.

5 • Pardon, monsieur, c'est ouvert le dimanche?
  • **On ouvre le matin** de neuf heures à midi trente mais c'est **fermé l'après-midi**.

6 • Pardon, monsieur, le château est ouvert le dimanche?
  • Oui, oui. Le château est ouvert **tous les jours de 9 h 30 à 19 h**.
  • Et le musée?
  • Le musée est ouvert **de 10 h à midi et de 14 h à 18 h** tous les jours **sauf le mardi**.

Page 74 Enquiring about timetables

2 • À quelle heure part le prochain train
pour Perpignan?
• À 14 h 25, madame. Et il arrive à
14 h 45.
• Et après?
• Il y a un train à **15 h 05**. Il arrive à
15 h 25. Puis il y a un train à 15 h 45.
• À quelle heure est-ce qu'il arrive?
• À **16 h 06**.
• Merci, monsieur.

3 • À quelle heure part le prochain train
pour Port-Vendres?
• Il y a un train à midi trente mais la
gare est loin. Il y a aussi **un car,
place du Marché**. C'est juste là,
en face.
• À quelle heure part le prochain car?
• **À midi.**
• Merci beaucoup, madame.

Page 75 Checking travel details

2

a • Je voudrais **un aller retour** pour
Perpignan, s'il vous plaît.
b • Un aller retour **en première**, s'il
vous plaît.
c • C'est quel quai?
• **Quai numéro 7**.
d • Il faut changer?
• Oui, il faut changer **à Marseille.**

3 a Je voudrais un aller simple en
seconde/en deuxième classe pour
Paris, s'il vous plaît.
b Je voudrais deux aller retour pour
Nice en seconde/en deuxième classe,
s'il vous plaît.
c Je voudrais un aller simple pour
Calais en première classe, s'il vous
plaît.

Page 76 Put it all together

1 a Je voudrais un aller simple pour Paris;
b Un aller-retour pour Nice, s'il vous

plaît; c À quelle heure part le prochain
train? d Le train part à midi quinze;
e Il faut changer à Lyon.

2 a changer; b faut; c retour; d ouvrez

3 a closed on Wednesdays; b Open
every day except Thursday; c English
spoken here

4 a Il faut réserver?
b Il faut changer à Paris?
c Il faut aller à Port-Vendres?

Page 77 Now you're talking!

1 • **Bonjour, madame. À quelle
heure part le prochain train
pour Boulogne?**
• À 15 h 15.
• **À quelle heure est-ce qu'il
arrive?**
• À 18 h 50.
• **Vous pouvez parler plus
lentement, s'il vous plaît?**
• Oui. À 18 h 50.
• **Il faut changer?**
• Oui. Il faut changer à Paris.
• **Je voudrais un aller simple, en
seconde.**
• Voilà, monsieur.
• **C'est combien?**
• Ça fait 32,90 €.
• **C'est quel quai?**
• Quai 6.

2 • **Bonjour, monsieur.**
• Ah, bonjour.
• **À quelle heure vous ouvrez?**
• À 6 h 30.
• **À quelle heure vous fermez?**
• On ferme de 13 h à 15 h.
• **C'est ouvert le dimanche?**
• Dimanche matin, oui, mais pas
dimanche après-midi.
• **Je ne comprends pas. Vous
pouvez répéter, s'il vous plaît?**
• Dimanche matin c'est ouvert, mais
dimanche après-midi, c'est fermé.

1 closed on Sundays; *2* midday; *3* you might have to pay a fine; *4* a coach; *5* huit heures; *6* jeudi; *7* every day; *8* you have to pay extra.

Unit 9 **Je voudrais du fromage, s'il vous plaît**

Pages 80 & 81 **Buying food and drink and asking for more (or less)**

2 • Alors, je voudrais du pain, de la confiture, du beurre, du thé, **du fromage**, du jambon, de la viande et des œufs.

3 • Je voudrais cinq croissants.
• Vous voulez des croissants au beurre ou nature?
• **Au beurre**, s'il vous plaît.

4 • Je voudrais du pain, de la confiture et des œufs.

6 *a* • Madame, vous désirez?
• Je voudrais du gruyère, s'il vous plaît.
b • Comme ça?
• Un peu plus, s'il vous plaît.
c • Voilà. Et avec ceci?
• Du roquefort, s'il vous plaît.
d • Comme ça?
• Un peu moins.
e • Bien. Et avec ça?
• Ce sera tout, merci.

7 • Je voudrais du brie, s'il vous plaît.
• Oui. Comme ça?
• **Un peu plus**, s'il vous plaît.
• Et avec ça?
• Je voudrais **du gruyère**.
• Du gruyère. . . Comme ça?
• Très bien.
• Et avec ceci?
• Ce sera tout, merci.

8 For example: du brie, du camembert, du Boursin, du gruyère, etc.

Page 82 **Saying how much you need**

2 • Je voudrais 250 grammes de fraises, un kilo de pommes, une livre de champignons, une demi-livre de tomates, un kilo de bananes, trois livres de pêches et un kilo de pommes de terre, s'il vous plaît.

3 • Je voudrais **une boîte de sardines**.
• Voilà, madame. Et avec ceci?
• **250 grammes de gruyère**, s'il vous plaît.
• 250 grammes de gruyère . . .
• Je voudrais aussi **une tranche de pâté**.
• Comme ça?
• Très bien . . . Et **quatre tranches de jambon** et **un kilo de pêches**.
• Voilà, madame. Avec ceci?
• Ce sera tout, merci.

Page 83 **Buying stamps and newspapers**

2 • Pardon, madame. Vous vendez des journaux anglais?
• Des journaux anglais? **Demain matin**, monsieur.

3 • C'est joli! C'est combien?
• **28,85 €**, monsieur.
• Oh, c'est **trop cher**.

4 • Alors, je prends juste les cartes postales et...vous vendez des timbres?
• Oui. Des timbres pour l'Angleterre?
• Oui. Quatre timbres, s'il vous plaît. Ça fait combien?
• Alors quatre cartes postales à un euro et quatre timbres à quarante-six centimes, ça fait cinq euros quatre-vingt-quatre, monsieur.
• C'est cher...euh...je prends juste deux cartes postales, alors.

- Très bien, monsieur. **Deux cartes postales** et deux timbres, ça fait **deux euros quatre-vingt-douze**. (**2,92 €**)

Page 84 Put it all together

1 - Bonjour, madame. Je **voudrais** du saucisson.
- Oui.
- Quatre **tranches** de celui-là.
- Quatre tranches de saucisson. Oui. Avec **ceci**, madame?
- Ce sera **tout**, merci.

2 - Je voudrais du pain, deux cent cinquante grammes de brie, une boîte de pâté, du beurre, trois tranches de jambon, un kilo de tomates, un kilo de bananes et deux bouteilles d'eau minérale.

3 a baker's; b newsagent's; c general food shop; d greengrocer's; e cheese shop

4 a fromage; b jambon; c croissant; d pommes

Page 85 Now you're talking!

1 - Vous désirez?
- **Je voudrais un kilo de pommes de terre.**
- Oui. Avec ceci?
- **Une demi-livre de pommes.**
- Voilà.
- **Vous vendez du jambon?**
- Oui.
- **Je voudrais quatre tranches de jambon, s'il vous plaît.**
- Très bien. Et avec ça?
- **Et du brie, s'il vous plaît.**
- Oui. Comme ça?
- **Un peu moins.**
- Voilà.
- **Et six œufs et une boîte de pâté.**
- Bien.
- **Ce sera tout. Ç'est combien?**
- Ça fait 8,50 €.

- **Voilà.**

2 - **C'est joli! Ç'est combien s'il vous plaît?**
- 36 euros.
- **C'est trop cher. Je prends les cartes postales.**
- Alors, deux cartes postales.
- **Vous vendez des timbres?**
- Oui. Alors deux cartes postales et deux timbres à 46 centimes.
- C'est combien?
- Ça fait 1,22 €.

Page 86 Quiz

1 pork and delicatessen foods; 2 yes; 3 des pommes de terre (potatoes); 4 1000; 5 French salami sausage; 6 no – it's too expensive; 7 a bit less; 8 no, you'd go to **le tabac** or **la poste**.

Unit 10 Bon appétit!

Page 88 Enquiring about snacks

2 - Qu'est-ce que c'est, un croque-madame?
- C'est **un croque-monsieur avec un œuf.**
- D'accord.

3 - Qu'est-ce que vous avez comme sandwichs?
- Sandwichs au saucisson, au jambon. . .
- Vous avez des sandwichs au fromage?
- Ah, non, monsieur.
- Alors, **un sandwich au saucisson, un sandwich au jambon**, et qu'est-ce que vous avez comme glaces?
- Glaces à la vanille, au chocolat, à la fraise, au citron . . .
- Alors, **une glace à la vanille et une glace au chocolat**, s'il vous plaît.
- D'accord.

Page 89 Reading a menu

2 • Thérèse, tu prends un menu ou à la carte?
• Je prends **le menu à 15 euros**.

She wants the set menu.

3 • Messieurs dames, vous avez choisi?
• Oui, le menu à 15 euros.
• Bien. Qu'est-ce que vous prenez comme entrées?
• Moi, je prends **la soupe à l'oignon**. Et toi, Thérèse?
• **Les moules au vin blanc**, s'il vous plaît.
• Et moi, **les crudités**.

Page 90 Ordering a meal

2 • Et comme plat principal?
• Moi, je prends le filet de porc normande.
• Pour moi, une entrecôte.
• Bien cuit, saignant, à point?
• Alors, moi, **bien cuit**, s'il vous plaît. Et toi, Philippe?
• Pour moi, **saignant**, s'il vous plaît.

3 • Et comme légumes, haricots verts, petits pois ou frites?
• **Haricots verts**, s'il vous plaît. Et toi, Fabien?
• **Des frites**, s'il vous plaît.
• Pour moi **une salade**, s'il vous plaît.
• Entendu.

4 • Et comme boisson?
• Une bouteille de vin rouge . . .
• Du bordeaux, du bourgogne, un côtes du rhône?
• Du **bordeaux**, s'il vous plaît. Et une carafe d'eau?
• Non, non. Une bouteille d'**eau gazeuse**, s'il vous plaît.

5 • Vous prenez un café?
• **Oui, merci. Trois cafés** et

l'addition, s'il vous plaît.
• Tout de suite, madame.

Page 91 Saying what you like and don't like

2 • Alors, Sabine, qu'est-ce que tu prends comme hors d'œuvre?
• Je n'aime pas les fruits de mer! Mais j'aime **la soupe à l'oignon**. Et toi?
• Moi, j'aime **les moules**. Et comme plat principal, qu'est-ce que tu prends: entrecôte ou poulet?
• Je prends **l'entrecôte**: j'aime la viande rouge.
• Moi, je n'aime pas la viande rouge: je prends **le poulet**.

3 • Mmmm . . . **le bœuf bourguignon** est **excellent**!
• Oui, c'est excellent!
• Et **le service** est **parfait**!
• Oui, parfait!
• Mais **le poulet rôti** n'est **pas bon**!
• **Le sorbet au cassis** est **très bon**. Et **le gâteau au chocolat**?
• Mmmmm . . . C'est **délicieux**! La **cuisine** est **excellente**.

4 For example: J'aime le poulet mais je n'aime pas les fruits de mer. J'aime les haricots verts et la salade. J'aime le vin rouge.

Page 92 Put it all together

a Le poulet rôti est excellent!; *b* Je prends un steak bien cuit, s'il vous plaît; *c* Qu'est-ce que vous avez comme sandwichs?; *d* Qu'est-ce que c'est, le bœuf bourguignon?; *e* Je n'aime pas les fraises; *f* Vanille, banane, chocolat, café, fraise ou cassis?; *g* Comme légumes, je prends des haricots verts.

2 avez; fraise; comme; tarte; prends

3 Qu'est-ce que vous avez comme . . .
a sandwichs? *b* omelettes? *c* glaces?

4 *Entrées:* moules, soupe, crudités
Viandes: poulet, bœuf, agneau
Légumes: petits pois, haricots verts, champignons
Desserts: glace, pommes, fraises

Page 93 **Now you're talking!**

1 • Bonjour . . . vous avez choisi?
 • **Deux menus à 15 euros, s'il vous plaît.**
 • Bien. Qu'est-ce que vous prenez comme entrées?
 • **Un pâté et une soupe.**
 • Et comme plat principal?
 • **Qu'est-ce que c'est un poulet basquaise?**
 • C'est du poulet cuit dans une sauce tomate avec des poivrons.
 • **Un poulet et un steak, s'il vous plaît.**
 • Steak saignant, à point ou bien cuit?
 • **À point.**
 • Bien. Et comme légumes?
 • **Des frites.**
 • Et comme boisson?
 • **Une bouteille de vin blanc et une bouteille d'eau gazeuse.**
 • Parfait.

2 • **Bon appétit!**
 • Merci. Toi aussi.
 • **Le poulet est délicieux!**
 • Mon steak est excellent!

 • Vous désirez du fromage ou un dessert?
 • **Qu'est-ce que vous avez comme glaces?**
 • Vanille, fraise, ou café.
 • **Une glace au café et un fromage.**

 • **Monsieur! Deux cafés et l'addition, s'il vous plaît.**

Page 94 **Quiz**

1 starter; *2* between 12 and 1.30; *3* no, he wants you to enjoy your meal; *4* the bill; *5* no, a strawberry tart; *6* a croque-madame is a croque-monsieur (cheese and ham toasted sandwich) served with a fried egg; *7* cheese or a dessert; *8* C'est délicieux!

Contrôle 3 (Pages 95–98)

1 b

2 c

3 • **Allez tout droit. Tournez à gauche et c'est la première rue à droite.**
 • C'est loin?
 • Non, c'est à **500 mètres.**

4
a Je voudrais une chambre pour deux personnes, s'il vous plaît.
 • Il y a seulement **une chambre avec deux lits et avec douche**. C'est la chambre **221** au **deuxième étage.**
b A twin room with shower; *c* 221;
d 2nd floor

5 *a* Local specialities, grilled fish and meat; *b* yes, it has air conditioning; *c* on Thursdays; *d* Monday.

6 • Et comme plat principal?
 • Un steak avec **des haricots verts** pour moi.
 • Le steak saignant, à point ou bien cuit?
 • **Saignant**, s'il vous plaît.
 • D'accord. Et pour monsieur?
 • Une entrecôte grillée avec **des frites.**
 • Et comme boisson?
 • **Une bouteille de vin rouge . . .** du bordeaux?
 • D'accord, et **une carafe d'eau.**

- Très bien. Une bouteille de bordeaux rouge et une carafe d'eau.

a rare; *b* green beans and chips; *c* red wine and a jug of water.

7 *a* every hour; *b* 50 minutes; *c* 10 p.m.; *d* 10–12 and 1.30–7 p.m.

8 *a* Je voudrais . . . du pain; une livre/cinq cents grammes de fromage; deux cents grammes de salami; trois tranches de jambon; six œufs; une bouteille de limonade; un kilo de pommes; une boîte de pâté; deux timbres.

9 *a* À quelle heure part le prochain train pour Paris? *b* À quelle heure (est-ce qu') il arrive? *c* Il faut changer? *d* Je voudrais un aller retour, s'il vous plaît.

10

a ● **Vous êtes français?**
   ● Non, je suis suisse.

b ● **Moi, je suis . . . Vous habitez où?**
   ● J'habite à la campagne.
c ● **Je m'appelle . . .**
   ● Enchanté. Philippe Pasquier.
d ● **Vous parlez anglais?**
   ● Non, je ne parle pas anglais.
e ● **Je suis . . . Et vous?**
   ● Je suis architecte.
f ● **Vous êtes marié?**
   ● Non. Je suis divorcé.
g ● **Vous avez des enfants?**
   ● Oui. J'ai une fille.
h ● **Elle a quel âge?**
   ● Elle a 14 ans.
i ● **Elle s'appelle comment?**
   ● Charlotte.

   ● Et vous, vous travaillez où?
   ● **Je travaille . . .**
   ● Et vous habitez en ville?
   ● **J'habite . . .**
   ● Vous êtes marié(e)?
   ● **Je suis . . .**
   ● Vous avez des enfants?
   ● **J'ai . . . / Je n'ai pas d'enfants.**

Grammar

Grammar is the term used to describe the patterns of a language. Knowing these patterns will enable you to move away from total reliance on set phrases.

1   **Nouns** (the words for people, things, places, concepts) are all either masculine (m.) or feminine (f.) in French. You need to know whether a noun is masculine or feminine in order to use the right word for 'the', 'a' and 'some', and the right form of adjectives.

As in English, most nouns add **-s** in the plural:

un enfant	**deux enfants**
une fille	**trois filles**

. . . but there are exceptions, including words ending in:

-s	**un fils**	**deux fils**
-eau	**un château**	**trois châteaux**
-al	**un journal**	**des journaux**

2   **Articles** (the, a/an, some) have various forms.

	a	the	some/any
singular (m.)	**un café**	**le café**	**du café**
singular (f.)	**une bière**	**la bière**	**de la bière**
before a vowel		**l'eau**	**de l'eau**
plural		**les pommes**	**des pommes**

'Some' and 'any' are often missed out in English, but never in French:

Vous avez des journaux anglais?
Do you have (any) English newspapers?

When 'any' is linked with 'not' you use **ne . . . pas de/d'**:

Il n'y a pas de pain.	There isn't any bread.
Je n'ai pas d'enfants.	I don't have any children.

3　**Adjectives** (words which describe) have to 'agree' with what they describe – the ending changes according to whether the noun is masculine or feminine, singular or plural. Usually, the feminine adds **-e** to the masculine and the plural form adds **-s**.

	masculine	feminine
singular	**le château est ouvert**	**la piscine est ouverte**
plural	**les magasins sont ouverts**	**les banques sont ouvertes**

Unlike in English, most adjectives generally come *after* the noun in French:

un vin italien an Italian wine　　**une ville anglaise** an English town

But a few common adjectives come before: **petit** (little), **grand** (big), **beau** (beautiful), **bon** (good) and ordinal numbers **premier** (first), **deuxième** (second), etc.

un grand hôtel a big hotel　　　**une petite ville** a small town

4　**De** (of) is used when talking about possession/belonging. There is no French equivalent of the English possessive 's:

la sœur de Pierre　　　　　Pierre's sister
le parking de la mairie　　　the town hall car park

de and **le** combine as **du**; **de** and **les** as **des**:

le parking du restaurant　　the restaurant car park
le parking des résidents　　the residents' car park

5　**À** can mean 'at' or 'to' and is also used:

to say what price something is:
un timbre à 50 centimes　　a 50-centime stamp
to talk about flavours or ingredients:
une glace à la vanille　　　a vanilla ice cream

à and **le** combine as **au**; **à** and **les** as **aux**:
un sandwich au jambon　　a ham sandwich
la tarte aux abricots　　　apricot tart

6 **Verbs** (words for doing or being) are easy to recognise in English because you can put 'to' in front of them – to live, to work, to be, to have. French verbs are listed in a dictionary in the infinitive form, ending in **-er**, **-ir** or **-re**. Verbs ending in **-er**, e.g. **aimer**, **habiter**, **parler**, **travailler**, **réserver**, all follow the same pattern, with different endings depending on *who* is doing something.

habiter (to live)	
I live	**j'habite**
you live	**tu habites**
he/she lives	**il/elle habite**
we live	**nous habitons**
you live	**vous habitez**
they live	**ils/elles habitent**

7 **Tu** and **vous** both mean 'you'. Use . . .
tu when talking to a friend, young person or relative
vous when talking to an adult who is not a close friend, or to more than one person.

8 **On** is often used instead of **nous** to mean 'we'. The verb which follows has the same verb ending as for **il** and **elle**.

On ferme à midi/Nous fermons à midi   We close at midday.

9 **Irregular verbs** are verbs which do not follow the pattern and have to be learnt separately. The following are common examples:

	avoir to have	**être** to be	**pouvoir** can/may	**vouloir** to want
je/j'	ai	suis	peux	veux
tu	as	es	peux	veux
il/elle	a	est	peut	veut
nous	avons	sommes	pouvons	voulons
vous	avez	êtes	pouvez	voulez
ils/elles	ont	sont	peuvent	veulent

	partir to leave	prendre to take	aller to go	faire to do/make
je	pars	prends	vais	fais
tu	pars	prends	vas	fais
il/elle	part	prend	va	fait
nous	partons	prenons	allons	faisons
vous	partez	prenez	allez	faites
ils/elles	partent	prennent	vont	font

10   Verbs following **pouvoir**, **vouloir** and **il faut** (it's necessary to) are always in the infinitive:

Je peux téléphoner?   Can I telephone?
Vous voulez partir?   Do you want to leave?
Il faut réserver.   You have to book.

11   To say something negative, **ne** goes in front of the verb and **pas** after:

Je n'aime pas les fruits de mer.   I don't like seafood.
Vous n'êtes pas d'ici?   You're not from here?

12   To change a statement into a question, you can either put **est-ce que** in front of it or simply change the way you say it so that it *sounds* like a question:

Do you speak English?
Vous parlez anglais?
Est-ce que vous parlez anglais?

Is there a garage near here?
Il y a un garage près d'ici?
Est-ce qu'il y a un garage près d'ici?

French–English glossary

This glossary contains only those words and phrases, and their meanings, as they occur in *Talk French*. Parts of irregular verbs are given in the form in which they occur, usually followed by the infinitive in brackets.

A

a (avoir) *(he/she) has (to have)*
à *to, at, with*
à l', à la, au, aux *to the, at the, in the*
l' abricot (m.) *apricot*
d' accord *OK*
l' addition (f.) *bill*
l' adresse (f.) *address*
l' âge (m.) *age*
l' agneau (m.) *lamb; la côte d'agneau lamb cutlet*
ai (avoir) *(I) have (to have)*
aider *to help*
aimer *to like, to love*
l' alimentation (f.) *grocery shop*
l' Allemagne (f.) *Germany*
allemand(e) *German*
aller *to go*
l' aller simple (m.) *single ticket*
l' aller retour (m.) *return ticket*
allez (aller) *(you) go (to go)*
alors *then, so, well, now*
américain(e) *American*
l' ami (m.) *friend, boyfriend*
l' amie (f.) *friend, girlfriend*
l' an (m.) *year*
ans *years*
anglais(e) *English*
l' Angleterre (f.) *England*
l' année (f.) *year*

l' anniversaire (m.) *birthday; joyeux anniversaire happy birthday!*
août (m.) *August*
l' apéritif (m.) *aperitif*
l' appartement (m.) *flat*
m'appelle (s'appeler) *(I) am called (to be called)*
appétit *appetite; bon appétit enjoy your meal*
après *after, afterwards*
l' après-midi (m.) *afternoon, in the afternoon*
l' architecte (m./f.) *architect*
l' arrivée (f.) *arrival*
arriver *to arrive*
as (avoir) *(you) have (to have)*
assez *enough, rather*
l' assiette (f.) *plate, platter; une assiette de crudités selection of raw vegetables*
aujourd'hui *today*
au revoir *goodbye*
l' Australie (f.) *Australia*
australien(ne) *Australian*
l' autoroute (f.) *motorway*
autre *other*
avant *before*
avec *with*
l' avenue (f.) *avenue*
avez (avoir) *(you) have (to have)*
avril (m.) *April*

B

la baguette *'stick' of bread*
la banane *banana*
la banque *bank*
beau (m.) *beautiful;*
le beau-frère *brother-in-law*
le beau-père *father-in-law*
beaucoup (de) *much, many, a lot (of)*
belle (f.) *beautiful*
la belle-mère *mother-in-law*
la belle-sœur *sister-in-law*
le beurre *butter; au beurre with butter*
bien *well*
la bière *beer*
le billet *ticket (train etc.)*
la billetterie *ticket service*
blanc(he) *white*
le bœuf *beef; bœuf bourguignon beef in red wine sauce*
la boisson *drink*
la boîte *tin, box*
bon(ne) *good; bonne chance good luck; bonne nuit goodnight*
bonjour *hello*
bonsoir *good evening; goodbye*
la boucherie *butcher's shop*
la boulangerie *baker's shop*
la bouteille *bottle*
bravo! *well done!*
le brie *Brie (cheese)*
le bureau *office; bureau de tabac tobacconist's*
le bus *bus; en bus by bus*

C

c', *it;* c'est *it is*

ça *that, it;* ça va *it's/I'm fine, OK;* ça va? *how are you? is it all right?;* ça fait? *that'll be . . .;* comme ça *like that*

la cabine *cabin;* cabine téléphonique *telephone box*

le café *coffee, café;* le café crème, le café au lait *white coffee, coffee with milk;* un grand café *a large coffee*

le camembert *Camembert (cheese)*

la campagne *country(side)*

le camping *campsite*

le Canada *Canada;* Canadien(ne) *Canadian*

le car *coach;* en car *by coach*

la carafe *jug, pitcher*

la carotte *carrot*

la carte *map, card, menu;* carte de crédit *credit card*

la carte postale *postcard*

le cassis *blackcurrant*

ce, cette *this;* ce soir *tonight*

ceci *this;* avec ceci? *anything else?*

cela *that*

célibataire *single*

celui-là *that one*

cent *hundred*

le cent *cent (100 = 1 euro)*

le centime *French currency*

le centre *centre;* le centre-ville *the town/city centre*

la cerise *cherry*

la chambre *bedroom, hotel room;* chambre d'hôtes

bed and breakfast

le champagne *champagne;* une bouteille de champagne *a bottle of champagne*

changer *to change*

la charcuterie *cold meats, pork butcher's*

le chat *cat*

le château *castle*

chaud(e) *hot*

cher/ère (m./f.) *dear, expensive;* trop cher *too expensive*

chez *at the home, company of;* chez moi *at home*

le chocolat *chocolate*

au chômage *unemployed*

choisir *to choose*

le cinéma *cinema*

cinq *five*

cinquante *fifty*

cinquième *fifth*

le citron *lemon*

la classe *class;* en première, seconde classe *(in) first, second class*

climatisé(e) *air-conditioned*

le coca *coke*

combien (de) *how much, how many;* c'est combien? *how much is it?*

comme *like, as, in the way of;* comme ça *like that*

comment *how;* comment tu t'appelles? *what's your name?;* comment vous appelez-vous? *what's your name?*

le commissariat *police station*

la compagnie *company*

complet (m.) *complete, full;* nous sommes complets *we're full up*

complète (f.) *complete, full*

composter *to punch, to stamp (ticket)*

comprendre *to understand, include;* je ne comprends pas *I don't understand*

compris(e) *included*

le concert *concert*

confirmer *to confirm*

la confiture *jam*

continuer *to continue, keep on*

le contrôle *checkpoint*

le côté *side;* à côté de *next to*

la côte *cutlet*

la côtelette *cutlet*

le cousin *male cousin*

la cousine *female cousin*

le crédit *credit;* la carte de crédit *credit card*

la crème *cream*

la crémerie *cheese shop*

le croissant *croissant;* croissants nature *ordinary croissants;* croissants au beurre *croissants made with butter*

le croque-madame *toasted ham and cheese sandwich with a fried egg*

le croque-monsieur *toasted ham and cheese sandwich*

les crudités (f.) *raw vegetables*

la cuisine *cooking*

cuit(e) *cooked;* bien
cuit(e) *well done*

D

d', de, du, de la, des *of,
from, some, any*
d'accord *OK, agreed*
dans *in, into*
la date *date*
décembre *December*
le déjeuner *lunch*
délicieux *delicious*
demain *tomorrow*
demi(e) *half*
dentiste (m./f.)
dentist
le départ *departure*
départemental(e)
departmental
le département
*department
(administrative area)*
désirer *to want;* vous
désirez? *What would
you like?*
le dessert *dessert*
deux *two*
deuxième *second*
dimanche *Sunday*
le dimanche *on Sundays,
every Sunday*
direct(e) *direct*
le directeur *manager,
director*
la direction *direction*
la distance *distance*
divorcé(e) *divorced*
dix *ten*
dix-huit *eighteen*
dix-neuf *nineteen*
dix-sept *seventeen*
donc *so, therefore*
la douche *shower*
douze *twelve*
droit(e) *right (-hand);*
tout droit *straight on;*
à droite *on, to the right*

la durée *duration*

E

l' eau (f.) *water;* eau
minérale *mineral water;*
eau gazeuse *sparkling
water*
écossais(e) *Scots,
Scottish*
l' Écosse (f.) *Scotland*
l' église (f.) *church*
elle *she*
elles *they (f.)*
l' emmenthal *Emmenthal
(cheese)*
en *in;* en face (de)
*opposite, facing you,
of them*
enchanté(e) *pleased to
meet you*
encore *yet, still*
l' enfant (m./f.) *child*
ensuite *then, next*
entre *between*
l' entrecôte (f.) *steak;*
entrecôte grillée *grilled
steak*
l' entrée (f.) *first course of
meal, starters*
environ *about,
approximately*
épeler *to spell*
es (être) *(you) are
(to be)*
l' escalope (f.) *escalope
(veal or pork fillet)*
l' Espagne (f.) *Spain*
espagnol(e) *Spanish*
est (être) *(he/she) is
(to be)*
est-ce que: est-ce qu'il y
a . . . ? *is/are there . . .*
et *and;* et vous?/et toi?
what about you?
l' étage (m.) *storey, floor;*
au premier étage *on
the 1st floor*

les États-Unis (m.) *United
States*
êtes (être) *(you) are
(to be)*
l' étudiant(e) *student*
l' euro (€) (m.) *euro
(European coin)*
exactement *exactly*
excellent(e) *excellent*
excuser *to excuse;*
excusez-moi *excuse
me, sorry*

F

F *abbreviation for* franc
en face (de) *opposite,
facing you*
faire *to do, to make;*
ça fait *that comes to*
la famille *family*
fantastique *fantastic*
il faut *it is necessary,
you/we/one must*
faux *false;* faux ami
false friend
la femme *wife*
ferme (fermer) *(it)
closes (to close)*
fermé(e) *closed*
fermez (fermer) *(you)
close (to close)*
février *February*
la fille *girl, daughter*
le fils *son*
finir *to finish, to stop*
fleuriste (m./f.) *florist*
la fraise *strawberry*
français(e) *French*
la France *France*
le frère *brother*
les frites (f.) *chips*
le fromage *cheese*
le fruit *fruit;* les fruits de
mer *seafood*

G

gallois(e) *Welsh*
le garage *garage*
la gare *station; gare SNCF
railway station*
le gâteau *cake*
gauche *left*, à gauche
on/to the left
gazeuse *sparkling;* eau
gazeuse *sparkling
water*
le gîte *rented house*
la gendarmerie *police
station*
la glace *ice, ice cream*
le gramme *gram*
grand(e) *big, large*
la grand-mère
grandmother
le grand-père *grandfather*
la Grande-Bretagne *Great
Britain*
griller *to grill*
le gruyère *Gruyère (cheese)*

H

habiter *to live*
le haricot *bean;* le haricot
vert *green bean*
l' heure (f.) *hour*
l' hôpital (m.) *hospital*
le hors-d'œuvre *starters*
l' hôtel (m.) *hotel*
l' hôtel de ville *town hall*
huit *eight*

I

ici *here;* d'ici *from here*
il *he, it*
il y a *there is, there are*
ils (m.) *they*
l' infirmier/ère (m./f.) *nurse*
l' ingénieur (m.) *engineer*
irlandais(e) *Irish*
l' Irlande (f.) *Ireland*

J

j', je *I*
le jambon *ham*
janvier *January*
le jardin *garden*
jeudi *Thursday*
le jeudi *on Thursdays,
every Thursday*
joli(e) *pretty, nice*
le jour *day*
le journal *newspaper*
juillet *July*
juin *June*
le jus *juice;* le jus de fruits
fruit juice
juste *just, correct*

K

le kilo *kilo*
le kilomètre *kilometre*

L

l', la, le, les *the*
là *there;* là-bas *over there*
le lait *milk*
le légume *vegetable*
lentement *slowly*
la limonade *lemonade*
le lit *bed;* un grand lit
a double bed; deux lits
two (twin) beds
la livre *pound, half-kilo*
la location *booking hire*
loin *far away;* loin
d'ici *far from here*
Londres *London*
lundi *Monday;* le lundi
*on Mondays, every
Monday*

M

m', me *me, myself*
M. *Mr*
ma, mes, mon *my*
madame *Mrs, madam*
mademoiselle *Miss*
le magasin *shop*

le magasin de fruits et
légumes *greengrocers'*
magnifique *magnificent*
mai *May*
maintenant *now*
la mairie *town hall*
mais *but*
la maison *house*
le marchand de journaux
newsagent's
le marché *market*
mardi *Tuesday*
le mardi *on Tuesdays,
every Tuesday*
le mari *husband*
marié(e) *married*
mars *March*
le matin *morning, in the
morning*
le médecin *doctor*
meilleur(e) *better;*
meilleures salutations
best wishes
le menu *set menu*
la mer *sea*
merci *thank you*
mercredi *Wednesday*
le mercredi *on
Wednesdays, every
Wednesday*
la mère *mother;* mère de
famille *housewife*
les messieurs *gentlemen*
le mètre *(abb. m) metre*
le métro *underground
railway*
midi *midday, noon*
mille *thousand*
minéral(e) *mineral;*
eau minérale *mineral
water*
minuit *midnight*
la minute *minute*
Mlle *Miss*
Mme *Mrs*
moi *me, myself;*
moi aussi *me too*

moins *less*
le mois *month*
monsieur *Mr, sir*
monsieur dame;
messieurs dames *ladies and gentlemen*
la moule *mussel*; moules au vin blanc *mussels in white wine*
le musée *museum*
la musique *music*

N

national(e) *national*;
la nationalité *nationality*
nature *plain*
ne/n'. . . pas *not*
ne/n'. . . pas de *no, not any*
ne/n'. . . plus *no more, no longer*
neuf *nine*
le nom *name, surname*
non *no*
nous *we*
novembre *November*
la nuit *night, at night*

O

octobre *October*
l' œuf (m.) *egg*
l' office du tourisme *tourist office*
l' omelette (f.) *omelette*
on *we, one, they*
ont (avoir) *(they) have (to have)*
onze *eleven*
l' orange (f.) *orange*
l' Orangina (m.) *fizzy orange drink*
ou *or*
où *where*
oui *yes*
ouvert(e) *open*
ouvre (ouvrir) *(it) opens (to open)*

ouvrez (ouvrir) *(you) open (to open)*

P

le pain *bread*
la panne *breakdown*;
en panne *broken down*
par *by, per*; par personne *per person*
le parc *park*
pardon *excuse me, pardon, sorry*
les parents (m.) *parents, relatives*
parfait(e) *perfect*
le parking *car park*
parler *to speak*
part (partir) *(it) leaves (to leave)*
partir *to leave*
pas *not*; pas de . . . *no . . . , not any . . .*
le pâté *pâté*
la pâtisserie *pastry (cake), cake shop*
payer *to pay*
le pays *country*
le pays de Galles *Wales*
le péage *toll*
la pêche *peach*
pendant *for*
le père *father*
la personne *person*
petit(e) *little, small*;
les petits pois *garden peas*
le petit déjeuner *breakfast*
peu *not much*; un peu (de) *a little (of)*; un peu moins *a bit less*; un peu plus *a bit more*
peux (pouvoir) *(I) can (to be able)*
la pharmacie *chemist's shop*
la piscine *swimming pool*
la pizza *pizza*

la pizzeria *pizzeria*
la place *square (open space in town)*
la plage *beach*
plaire *to please*;
s'il vous plaît *please*
le plat *dish*; des plats végétariens *vegetarian dishes*
le plateau *platter*
plus *more*; un peu plus *a little bit more*
le point *point*; à point *medium (steak)*
le poisson *fish*
la pomme *apple*
la pomme de terre *potato*
le pont *bridge*
le porc *pork*; le filet de porc *loin of pork*
le porto *port*
la porte *door*
possible *possible*
la poste *post office*
le poulet *chicken*
pour *for, (in order) to*;
pour aller à/au . . . ? *to get to . . . ?*; pour moi *for me*
pouvez (pouvoir) *(you) can (to be able)*
pouvoir *to be able, can*
premier/ère (m./f.) *first*
prendre *to take, have*
prends (prendre) *(I) take, have (to take, have)*
prenez (prendre) *(you) take, have (to take, have)*
le prénom *first name*
près *near*; près de *near (to)*; près d'ici *near here*
la pression *draught beer*
principal(e) *main*,
le plat principal *main dish/course of meal*
privé(e) *private*
le prix *price*

prochain(e) *next*
le professeur *teacher*
la profession *job*
la promenade *trip;*
    promenade en mer
    boat trip
la propriété *house,*
    property
    proposer *to propose,*
    to suggest
    puis *then*

Q

qu', que *that, than, what,*
    which
le quai *railway platform*
    quand . . . ? *when . . . ?*
    quarante *forty*
    quatorze *fourteen*
    quatre *four*
    quatre-vingt-dix *ninety*
    quatre-vingts *eighty*
    quatrième *fourth*
    quel, quelle *what,*
    what a . . . , which; à
    quelle heure? *at what*
    time?
    qu'est-ce que . . . ?
    what . . . ?; qu'est-ce
    que c'est? *what is it?*
    qui *which, who, whom*
la quiche *flan*
    quinze *fifteen*

R

la région *region*
    régional(e) *regional*
le(s) renseignement(s) (m.)
    information
    répéter *to repeat*
la réservation *booking*
    réserver *to reserve, to*
    book
les résidents *residents*
le restaurant *restaurant*
    retraité(e) *retired*

la rivière *river*
le roquefort *French cheese*
    rôti(e) *roast*
    rouge *red*
la route *road;* route
    nationale *main road;*
    route départementale
    small road
la rue *street, road*

S

s', se, ses *himself, herself,*
    itself
    s' *if (in front of vowel or 'h')*
    sa, ses, son *his, her, its*
    saignant(e) *rare (steak)*
la salade *(green) salad,*
    lettuce
la salle *room, hall;*
    la salle de bains
    bathroom
le salon de thé *teashop*
    salut! *hi! bye!*
les salutations *greetings,*
    wishes; meilleures
    salutations *best wishes*
    samedi *Saturday;*
    le samedi *on Saturdays,*
    every Saturday
le sandwich *sandwich*
    sans *without*
la santé *health;* à votre
    santé! *good health!*
    cheers!
la sardine *sardine*
la sauce *sauce*
le saucisson *salami*
    sauf *except*
    second(e) *second;*
    en seconde (classe)
    (in) second class
    secrétaire (m./f.)
    secretary
    seize *sixteen*
la semaine *week*
    sept *seven*

septembre *September*
    sera (être) *(it/that) will*
    be (to be); ce sera tout?
    will that be all?
le service *service, service*
    charge
    seulement *only*
    si *if*
    six *six*
la SNCF *French National*
    Railways
la sœur *sister*
le soir *evening;* ce soir
    this evening
    soixante *sixty*
    soixante-dix *seventy*
    sommes (être) *(we) are*
    (to be)
    sont (être) *(they) are;*
    (to be)
le sorbet *sorbet*
la soupe *soup;* soupe à
    l'oignon *onion soup*
la spécialité *speciality*
le steak *steak*
    suis (être) *(I) am (to be)*
    suisse *Swiss*
la Suisse *Switzerland*
le supermarché
    supermarket
le supplément *extra charge*
    sur *on*
    sûr(e) *sure;* bien sûr
    of course

T

t', te *you, yourself*
    ta, ton, tes *your*
le tabac *tobacconist's shop*
la table *table*
la tarte *tart, pie;* tarte
    maison *home-made pie*
le taxi *taxi*
le téléphone *telephone*
    téléphoner *to telephone*
la télévision *television*

terminer *to finish*

la terrasse *terrace*

le TGV (train à grande vitesse) *high-speed train*

le thé *tea (drink);* le thé au citron *lemon tea;* le thé nature *black tea;* le thé au lait *tea with milk*

le timbre *postage stamp*

toasté *toasted*

toi *you, yourself*

les toilettes (f.) *toilet*

la tomate *tomato*

toujours *always, still*

tourner *to turn*

tous, tout, toute *all, everything*

tous les jours *every day*

tout de suite *right away;* toutes les heures *every hour*

toutes directions *all directions*

le train *train*

la tranche *slice*

le transport *transport;* transport maritime *sea transport*

le travail *work, job*

travailler *to work*

treize *thirteen*

trente *thirty*

très *very;* très bien *very well, fine*

trois *three*

troisième *third*

trop *too*

se trouver *to be situated*

tu (sing.) *you*

U

un, une *a, an, one*

V

va (aller) *(it) goes (to go);* ça va? *how's it going?* ça va *it's OK/I'm fine*

la vanille *vanilla*

varié(e) *varied, various*

végétarien(ne) *vegetarian*

vendre *to sell*

vendredi *Friday;* le vendredi *on Fridays, every Friday*

venir *to come*

le verre *glass*

vert(e) *green*

veuf, veuve *widowed*

la viande *meat;* la viande rouge *red meat*

vient (venir) *(he/she) comes (to come)*

le village *village*

la ville *town, city;* en ville *in (a) town*

le vin *wine;* vin rouge *red wine;* vin blanc *white wine*

vingt *twenty*

voici *here is/are, here you are*

voilà *there is/are, there you are*

la voiture *car, carriage*

votre, vos *your*

voudrais (vouloir) *(I) 'd like (to want, to wish);* vous voulez *do you want . . . ?*

vouloir *to want, to wish*

vous (pl.) *you*

vrai(e) *true, real*

vraiment *really*

la vue *view*

W

les WC (m.) *toilet, WC*

Y

y *there;* il y a *there is, there are;* il y en a *there are some of them;* il y en a (un/une) (m./f.) *there is (one of them)*

Z

zéro *nought*

Keep on talking!

If you're keen to progress to a higher level, BBC Languages offers a wide range of innovative products, from short courses and grammars to build up your vocabulary and confidence, to more in-depth courses for beginners or intermediates. Designed by language-teaching experts, our courses make the best use of today's technology, with book and audio, audio-only and multimedia products on offer. Many of these courses are accompanied by free online activities at www.bbc.co.uk/languages, and television series, which are regularly repeated on the BBC TWO Learning Zone.

Beginner

Travel

Beginner

Intermediate

Resources

For more information on the BBC Languages range visit: www.bbclanguages.com. For a catalogue, call: (020) 8433 3135.

BBC books are available from bookshops, or direct from Bookpost on (01624) 675137. Or order online at: www.bbclanguages.com.